The Afterlife Evidence

The Afterlife Evidence

Comforting and Convincing Proof That No One Really Dies

by Mark Pitstick MA, DC

Waterside Productions

Printed in the United States of America
First Printing, 2022

ISBN-13: 978-1-956503-59-3 print edition
ISBN-13: 978-1-956503-60-9 ebook edition

Waterside Productions
2055 Oxford Ave
Cardiff, CA 92007
www.waterside.com

DEDICATION

To Andy whose evolved nature helped me realize and fine-tune my own.

To my material and postmaterial family and friends who have given me so much love and support.

To my patients over the last 50 years who have taught me so much that schools never could.

To my colleagues in the afterlife and consciousness field – especially Dr. Gary Schwartz – who have taught me so much while validating my beliefs and findings.

To my spiritual support team – angels, guides, master teachers, soulmates, and more – who love, support, assist and guide me always.

To E.L.G.O.D. – the energizing, loving, guiding, organizing, and designing Presence and Power of which we each are integral, infinite, eternal, and beloved parts.

Dedication

Table of Contents

Introduction

Starting at age 19 in 1972, I worked part-time for six years as a respiratory therapist during my pre-med and theological studies. By age 20, I was trained to draw arterial blood gas samples, insert endotracheal breathing tubes, assist in cardiopulmonary resuscitation, and set up and maintain ventilators.

One day, soon after my intensive training was over, I heard the *Code 4* life-threatening emergency alarm and ran to the emergency room. It was my first 'stat' call and I was ready to save lives.

Mikey, a five-year-old boy with blond hair, had been hit by a truck. As we worked on him, someone said he was an only child. Despite hours of our best efforts, he died from multiple injuries. In shock, I stumbled out into the hall and saw the parents' faces contort in grief as the lead doctor told them the news.

I went outside, shook my fist at the sky, and said: 'God, you SOB! At church, *I was taught you are all knowing, all loving, and all powerful.* If that's really true, why didn't you help Mikey? If you couldn't help him, you aren't all those things. And if you *could have helped him, but didn't,* what kind of twisted supposed Creator are you?'

A month later, I met Stevie. A two-year-old boy with big brown eyes and a sad smile, he was a frequent visitor to the pediatric ward. First a broken leg, then a broken arm, then fractured ribs. His mother and her boyfriend shrugged and said he was just a very active toddler. I felt sorry for the little guy and visited to play with him when I could.

One afternoon, I was paged to the ER for a Code 4 as the squad brought in a little boy who was in severe condition. I met the ambulance team as they brought him into the treatment room. They handed the little body to me and I put him on the table. I felt a slight tugging as I removed my hands from his bare back and, in horror, saw them covered with dead skin from his body.

It was Stevie.

The doctors couldn't find a pulse or good vein for an IV. His respirations were very shallow and he was severely dehydrated. There was nothing we could do and soon he passed on. Later, the back-story filtered in. It was reported that the mother wasn't home, and her boyfriend 'gave him a bath' in such hot water that Stevie literally cooked to death. Seeing this act of depravity – and realizing his past injuries probably weren't accidents – made life seem even more hopeless and meaningless.

Although I didn't realize it at the time, my search for afterlife evidence began then. Other professional and personal experiences made me search for meaningful answers to life's biggest questions. I'm sure you know the list. For me, these included: *Does life truly continue after the body dies? Will we really see our 'departed' loved ones again?*

I collected every piece of information I could find – pro or con – about the subject in a file folder. Twenty years later, when those article clippings and notes filled three boxes, I knew it was time to write a book. A spiral-bound volume at first, *Soul Proof* was sold to patients and attendees at talks I gave about spiritual awareness.

In 1995, 75-year-old Roberta was my first patient of the day. (I had relieved her migraines for years with specific chiropractic adjustments. During her visits, she shared that her husband was very ill so our conversations naturally led to the evidence for life after death.) That morning, her eyes were red and she looked very tired. I asked if she had been up all night with a migraine. Roberta replied that she didn't sleep well because her husband had passed on.

I gave my condolences and asked when that happened. *'Four hours ago'*, she said. I replied, 'Oh, Roberta, I'm so sorry. You didn't have to keep your appointment; we would certainly understand if you didn't even think to call under those circumstances.' She said, 'I know, that's what my family told me. But I told them that – at a time like this – there isn't anyone I would rather be with than Dr. Pitstick.'

That's when I fully realized my highest calling. After that, providing holistic health care became a part-time endeavor that allowed me to focus full time on spiritual awareness and afterlife topics. For the last 26 years, I've shared this evidence via books, articles, lectures, and radio shows as both a host and guest.

The answer to those two big questions above? *Does life truly continue after the body dies? Will we really see our 'departed' loved ones again?* ***Based on the collective evidence now available in 2021, the answers are clearly: YES and YES.***

A vast and varied amount of evidence – from firsthand experiences, clinical studies, and scientific research – now *irrefutably proves that life continues after death of the human form.*

I use the words 'proof' and 'prove' responsibly and accurately. A definition for proof from *Webster's Third New International Dictionary* includes: *"knowledge acquired by experience; something that induces certainty and establishes validity."* ***Based on this lay definition, proof of afterlife has been clearly shown.***

To accurately use the word 'proof' in a scientific context requires *replicated, double-blinded, controlled, multi-centered, and randomized-ordered experiments with highly statistically significant findings published in peer-reviewed scientific journals.* ***Based on this scientific definition, proof of afterlife has been definitively demonstrated.***

For the first time in human history, you can – without a doubt – know that ***life after death is real.*** This evidence also corroborates major religious and spiritual teachings over the millennia. You can now breathe a huge sigh of relief and release all fear that death is an end. Here's how Andrew put it in a recent note …

> "Just finished your book *The Eleven Questions.* Started reading and did NOT put it down until done. You and this afterlife information have given me a peace and calmness that I never expected nor thought possible. No longer do I wonder about life everlasting. I now KNOW it is there to be looked forward to. Now I know love never dies and neither did my dear wife. Thank you for helping me know this is true."

Overview of the Collective Evidence

The afterlife evidence will be presented in three categories: *firsthand experiences, clinical studies,* and *scientific research.* Definitions of each include:

1. ***Firsthand experiences*** are perceptions reported by the person having them.

2. ***Clinical studies*** involve data collected and analyzed by a university professor, physician, and / or psychologist in a professional office or hospital.

3. ***Scientific research*** includes findings from experiments performed by scientists in a university or institute lab using the criteria listed above.

You may personally be most convinced by one category or subcategory of evidence. *However, **the combination of all the evidence provides the strongest proof of life after death.***

Before presenting the evidence, a few remarks ...

1. I use single quotation marks around certain words because of their strongly anchored erroneous or limiting meanings. For example, some people use the words 'death, die, dead, deceased, and departed' to connote a permanent end of life.

2. I primarily use more accurate terms such as *pass on, change worlds, graduate from earth-school, cross over, and transition to the next phase of life.*

3. *Different word combinations* are used even though those are longer and may initially seem awkward. For example, instead of saying '*she* died', I will say *'her body* died.' ***I'm sure you can appreciate the difference.*** In this era of convincing proof that life continues after bodily death, it's important to clearly differentiate that *the woman didn't really die, just her no longer needed physical shell did.*

4. Superscript capital letters such as [A] and [B] indicate that additional information is provided in the *Resources* section at the end of this book.

5. *References* are noted by a number within parentheses, for example, (1).

6. I use the term ***postmaterial person*** to describe those whose outer form has died. It fits very well with current evidence that people who no longer live on *earth – the*

material world – continue to live in a *postmaterial realm*. These terms have been used for centuries in philosophical discussions about the nature of reality. Postmaterial is also a term adopted by the *Academy for Advancement of Postmaterialist Sciences*, a group of scientists, professors, physicians, and psychologists who consider consciousness to be a fundamental component of reality – not merely a temporary by-product of the brain. [A]

7. The terms *evidential, validated,* and *documented* describe afterlife evidence that has corroborating features.

8. To preserve anonymity, the names of real people who graciously provided very personal details about their lives have been changed.

We live in an exciting time when evidence about life after death is more widely available in books, articles, blogs, documentaries, and more. As such, ***this is a very comforting, inspiring, and hopeful time for humanity.***

I hope the information in this book adds to those resources, and helps you:

1. *Release* fear, hopelessness, anger, guilt, and other *lower-energy* emotions / ways of being associated with 'death and dying'.

2. Realize this earthly experience is a totally safe, meaningful, and magnificent adventure amidst forever.

3. Gain sensible answers about *apparent paradoxes*, for example, how a wise and loving Creator can coexist with suffering such as the death of a child [B].

4. *Experience* more peace, joy, love, hope, enthusiasm, compassion, enlightenment, gratitude, and other *higher-energy* emotions / ways of being.

Category 1
Evidence from Firsthand Experiences

Firsthand experience evidence is defined as afterlife-related perceptions reported by the person having them. Synonyms for this category include *empirical evidence* and *experiential evidence.*

Firsthand experiences are the least objective, but ***often the most personally meaningful*** indicators of life after death. Direct perceptions can pass the *seeing is believing* or, more accurately, *sensing is believing* test. Glimpses of *postmaterial persons* – again, the so-called 'deceased' – often occur when those living on earth are very relaxed, dreaming, near death, or in an altered state of consciousness.

Part of the brain's function is to *filter out* nonessential input. That was adaptive for survival, for example, while accurately distinguishing between edible and poisonous berries. However, that survival-focused level of perception may be maladaptive in the 21st century. Humans can only sense a very small fraction of reality. *Unless informed otherwise, **they may erroneously assume that only what can be perceived by the five senses is real.***

It's a scientific fact that the human brain and senses are very limited in perceiving reality. For example, humans usually can't hear a dog whistle, or differentiate between eight shades of white like hummingbirds can. What appears to earthly eyes as white light is really, as revealed by a simple prism, a rainbow of colors. The electromagnetic spectrum contains many wavelengths – gamma rays and x-rays, for example – that human senses cannot detect.

In her book *The Field*, science journalist Lynne McTaggart described the views of top quantum physicists about how little of reality people usually perceive. She summarized their input with this analogy: If all the light and energy in our world were the size of Mt. Everest, the average person could only sense a golf-ball sized portion of that.

This alone explains why more humans don't perceive postmaterial loved ones. *Most people have been fooled by their senses.* The old saying 'There is more to life than meets the eye' is quite accurate and extremely important to remember.

Relaxing your brain's judgments about 'what is real' and 'what is imaginary' is one key to expanding your awareness of the big picture of life. And that, in turn, can enable more frequent and meaningful relationships with your dear ones who have changed worlds. [C]

Methods for enhancing firsthand experiences of postmaterial persons are now widely available. ***A common thread among these approaches is expanding your awareness.*** I especially recommend meditation, prayer, setting intentions, yoga, breathwork, techniques using deep relaxation, shamanic journeying, and mind-expanding audio technology. [D]

Subcategories of firsthand experiences include: *after-death communications, out-of-body experiences, ghost sightings, spiritually transformative experiences, electronic voice projection / instrumental transcommunication, and other ways of knowing.*

After-Death Communications

After-death communication (ADC) is a term that describes meaningful contact, while awake or asleep, with postmaterial persons. *Waking* ADCs may involve the usual five senses, or more ethereal ones. The latter have been described as *seeing with the mind's eye, hearing telepathically,* or *having an inner knowing.* Dream ADCs often seem more vivid and real than usual ones. The dreamer awakens with ***a strong sense that actual contact was made.*** *A lasting peace* about the living presence and wellbeing of 'departed' loved ones is one indication that dream ADCs may be more than just wish fulfillment.

In the past, many people did not share their ADCs for fear of being considered weird or crazy. More people are now openly discussing these surprisingly common experiences. A National Opinion Research Center poll conducted by Father Andrew Greeley, PhD found that 42% of American adults and 67% of widows believe they have been in contact with postmaterial persons. (1) Informal surveys during my presentations to many bereaved parents reveal that *nearly all of them* have experienced one or more meaningful contacts with their children.

Evidential ADCs provide validation because people *learn something they did not know about or could not know about from a postmaterial person.* Detailed information from evidential ADCs provides stronger documentation that at least some ADCs are not imaginary. Visiting postmaterial persons have described long-lost objects that were subsequently discovered. They also have relayed specific information that apparently was not known to anyone, but was later verified. Several validation ADCs cases were described in *Hello from Heaven* by Bill Guggenheim and Judy Guggenheim.

In *Memories, Dreams, Reflections,* Carl Jung, MD reported the following evidential ADC:

> "One night I lay awake thinking of the sudden death of a friend whose funeral had taken place the day before. I was deeply concerned. Suddenly I felt that he was in the room. It seemed to me that he stood at the foot of my bed and was asking me to go with him.
>
> Then I said to myself, 'Proof is neither here nor there! Instead of explaining him away as a fantasy, I might just as well give him the benefit of the doubt and for experiment's sake credit him with reality.' The moment I had that thought, he went to the door and beckoned me to follow him."

Dr. Jung described following, *in his mind,* the friend to his house. In the study, his friend pointed to the second of five books with red bindings on the second shelf from the top. Said Jung:

> "I was not acquainted with his library and did not know what books he owned. Certainly, I could never have made out from below the titles of the books he had pointed out to me, on the second shelf from the top. This experience seemed to me so curious that the next morning I went to his widow and asked whether I could look up something in my friend's library. I stepped up on the stool so as to be able to read the titles. They were translations of the novels of Emile Zola. The title of the second volume read: *The Legacy of the Dead*." (2)

My dear friends Dottie and Joe Asselin were as close to 'earth-angels' as anyone I've met. I knew Joe, a retired engineer, for nearly twenty years until he passed on in 2013. In 2014, I asked Dottie, "Have you heard from Joe lately?" Without hesitating, she replied, "Oh sure, all the time." Then she told me about the following event ...

Shortly before he transitioned to the next phase of life, Joe completed their taxes for 2013 using *TurboTax®* software. He told Dottie, "If I'm not around in April when taxes are due, just enter this code and everything will print out for the accountant." Dottie was staying with her daughter Sue during the month before taxes were due. They couldn't find the code and feared they would have to start over.

That night, Dottie prayed that she wouldn't have to re-do the tax preparation. The next morning, her phone registered a text from Joe Asselin even though his account had been canceled. The message read: "the TurboTax code is" followed by a series of numbers. Dottie showed the message to Sue and they quickly entered the code into the tax preparation system. The work that Joe had completed successfully opened.

Soon afterwards, Dottie checked her phone but there was no record of that text. Sue, a physician and hospital administrator, checked the phone and couldn't find it either.

This is a remarkable ADC with both shared and evidential aspects. ('Shared' means that more than one person observed the same ADC.) It makes sense that someone like Joe could manipulate the functioning of electronic devices.

By the way, did you notice my language when I spoke with Dottie? Joe's body died the year before, and yet I asked her: 'Have you heard from Joe lately?' That's an example of *conscious language* you can now accurately and responsibly use since life after death has been proven.

Elisabeth Kubler-Ross, MD also had an evidentiary ADC. As related by Raymond Moody, MD, PhD in his book *Reunions*, Dr. Kubler-Ross was walking in the hallway toward her office one day and noticed a woman standing in the corridor. They talked a bit and, after a while, Dr. Ross said: 'I know you!' She recognized the woman as 'Mrs. Schwartz,' *a patient whose body had died several months earlier.* Mrs. Schwartz acknowledged her identity and the two talked for some time. In an attempt to obtain verifiable evidence of the visit, Kubler-Ross asked the woman to write a note to a minister who also helped the woman. Analysis of the postmaterial woman's handwriting matched samples written before she crossed over. (3)

Facilitated ADCs *involve methods to increase the chances of having meaningful contacts.* ADCs usually only occur spontaneously. Many people wish to receive signs from their loved ones, but that seems beyond conscious control. Fortunately, ***several approaches now exist to increase the chances of having an ADC***: the *Psychomanteum Mirror Gazing Technique, Induced After-Death Communications,* and *Facilitated ADC Technique.* [E]

As described in Dr. Moody's book *Reunions,* the psychomanteum involves mirror gazing in a totally quiet and nearly darkened room. Sensory deprivation and the mirror's clear optical depth assist perception of postmaterial loved ones. Validation cases have been reported after sessions led by therapists around the world. On one occasion, several subjects in a large mirror gazing booth saw the same apparition as confirmed by comparing notes afterward. (4)

I was certified in 2000 by Dr. Moody to do this work, and used it personally and with clients. Several validation aspects arose during a mirror gazing session with Chris and Catherine. For clinical objectivity, before the session we did not share who we hoped to contact.

Twenty minutes into the session, I saw a gauzy female figure forming in the bottom of my peripheral vision. It looked like someone at the halfway stage of getting beamed up on *Star Trek.* First an outline, then the interior partly filled in so I could see the figure of a female with long brown hair. I telepathically asked what name she went by. A thought impression of the names 'Mary' and 'Margaret' immediately registered, but my over-analyzing brain was skeptical.

I next silently asked the apparition who she came to visit and received the impression it was for Chris. "Well," my skeptical mind chimed in, "That's a 50-50 chance. (since those names were not meaningful for me) *How do you know you aren't just making all this up?*"

Just then, I felt a moderately forceful tap on my left shoulder, as if someone or something was saying: "*Uh-huh. Are you making THAT up?*"

Now, keep in mind, I set up the small room and *knew* no one else was in there. Through my peripheral vision, I could see Chris and Catherine sitting five feet away on either side of me. So I *knew* they didn't do it. Several minutes later, I felt another firm tap in the same place followed by a brisk rubbing along the lateral aspect of my left thigh. That quieted my skeptical mind.

After the session, we shared our experiences. When I mentioned the names I received and who they were for, Chris covered her mouth and exclaimed: "Margaret is my mother and Mary is my grandmother! That's who I hoped to contact." *I was very impressed by* seeing the gauzy form, getting touched three times, and receiving verifiable information that I did not know.

The *Induced ADC Technique* was described by Allan Botkin, PsyD and Craig Hogan, PhD in their book *Induced After-Death Communications.* Techniques using eye movement, desensitization, and reprocessing are used. This approach has been very successful with many clients and hundreds of trained psychotherapists have used it. The technique seems to work equally well whether people are religious or agnostic, and for recent as well as longer cases of grieving.

I designed the *Facilitated ADC Technique* after training from Drs. Brian Weiss, Raymond Moody, and Ken Ring that prepared me to create this novel approach. This method uses deep relaxation / hypnosis and guided imagery to quiet the over-analyzing brain. Participants often have meaningful perceptions of postmaterial loved ones. I have primarily used it with large groups of bereaved parents. Post-session 'show of hand' surveys show that about 75% of participants have meaningful perceptions during their first session. The parents describe seeing their children in solid or gauzy form, feeling their touch, hearing their voice, and knowing they are alive, whole, and happy.

Out-of-Body Experiences

Out-of-body experience is a term referring to a person's awareness leaving the body without being nearly dead. This can occur spontaneously, in meditative states, and during intense situations such as childbirth or imminent danger. Out-of-body experiences can also be facilitated during techniques designed for that purpose.

Out-of-body-experiences provide *personally meaningful experiences* that consciousness exists independently of the brain. There are also some documented aspects. Experiencers have reported visiting distant places and sensing verifiable details. *Remote viewing*, an accurate awareness of events and details in far-away places, has been investigated by the Stanford Research Institute.

Demonstrable physical effects during out-of-body experiences have been reported. Robert Monroe, founder of the Monroe Institute and author of *Journeys Outside of the Body*, shared the following example. To explore the effects of actions from afar, he gently pinched a friend who was visiting another country. Later, he asked if she had experienced any unexplainable events. She showed him a bruise where she had felt a rather forceful pinch. Monroe realized his gentle effort had been too much. To learn more, visit MonroeInstitute.org, and the Out of Body Experience Research Foundation (OBERF.org) of Jeffrey Long, MD and Jody Long, JD.

Several profound out-of-body experiences have occurred during *Holistic Breathwork* sessions I've led for many people in groups over the last 25 years. This technique involves forty minutes of open-mouthed, noisy, uninterrupted, diaphragmatic breathing. Different types of music and my coaching in the background serve to confound the brain and diminish its over-analyzing perceptual limitations.

For example, while doing the breathwork, a sixty-five-year-old female cried very hard for fifteen minutes while rolled up in a fetal position. She then became so still and quiet that I checked to see if she was still breathing. Afterward, I asked what she experienced. While crying, she felt much sadness and loneliness that had been her companions since her husband, parents, and several pets changed worlds. During the quiet time, however, *she experienced visiting them*. She told our group: 'I'm totally convinced that I really visited with them. It wasn't just a visualization.' Based on my observations of her during the session, and her deep peace afterwards, I considered that to be quite likely.

As mentioned, *intense emotions can trigger these experiences.* A ten-year-old girl who attended one of my workshops with her mother described an experience she had at age two. Her mom left her with a babysitter for the first time and gave clear instructions to attend to the child if she cried. The babysitter, however, ignored the crying child who eventually had a strange event.

Even though she couldn't see out the window from her crib, the little one could see *another version of herself* on the sidewalk below. This self-described *other part of herself* reassured the crying infant and said everything would be OK. The child's experience continued as her awareness floated into the living room and saw the babysitter there. She remembered the babysitter's appearance and the clothing she had on. Her mother verified the facts later reported when the daughter could verbalize. This ten-year-old seemed quite poised, calm, and wise beyond her years.

Shamanic and other indigenous spiritual practices can allow a person to experience life differently. Of this work, Michael Harner, PhD – anthropologist and author of *The Way of the Shaman* – stated: "After having personally practiced shamanism, shamanic healing, and shamanic journeying for more than half a century, I can say that there is nothing I have encountered in reports of the spiritual experiences of saints, prophets, psychedelic drug experimenters, near death survivors, avatars and other mystics that is not commonly experienced when following classic journey methods using a drum." (5)

Don, a longtime subscriber of my *Soul Proof* newsletter, shared the following. In this case, the therapist used a shamanic-mediated state to obtain significant information.

> "My father died when I was eleven months old, so I never really knew him. I do have several of his possessions including a tennis racquet that he used. I recently thought about where to store it and, during that time, I thought more and more about him. I scheduled a session with a Catholic nun who is a psychotherapist and uses shamanic techniques. My wife was with me. The therapist asked if a loved one who had died might assist her in spirit during the session. I gave her my dad's name.
>
> At the end of the session, she said my father's spirit was present and he had a gift for me. She described him holding out his hand with a tennis racquet in it! It was an older version, she said, not one you would find in a sporting goods store today. There was absolutely no way that the nun knew about the tennis racquet – none! I can only conclude that, somehow, my father was present and wanted to contact me with a sign that only my wife and I would understand." (6)

Skeptics could say the psychotherapist read Don's mind and picked up a meaningful experience about his dad. They are correct; that is a possibility that has to be considered. That's why Don's report is considered a firsthand experience – it couldn't be clinically or scientifically evaluated. However, hundreds of people have told me similar stories over the last 25 years. The sheer number of these experiential events, and their lasting impact on the people involved is impressive.

Ghost Sightings

Ghost sightings are another phenomenon that adds to the evidence that consciousness survives physical death. In the video documentary *Sightings: The Ghost Report*, paranormal researcher Tony Cornell of Cambridge University stated: "There's a lot of fraud in this, a lot of imagination, a lot of wishful thinking. But when you strip that all out, there's about 20% hard core stuff that's exceedingly difficult to explain." (7)

I use the term 'ghost' to describe postmaterial persons who, after bodily death, didn't fully transition from earth to an afterlife realm. Reasons for being 'stuck' may include: intense addictions, strong emotions such as revenge and anger, sudden or violent death, limited awareness about life after death, and / or fear about leaving the earth plane.

Being in this sort of netherworld sounds like purgatories described by some religious denominations. My understanding is that 'stuck souls' can enter the Light anytime they choose. Perhaps their temporary 'between worlds' experiences are adaptive for karmic or growth reasons, or to help others in ways we can't understand.

What, you may wonder, is *the difference between ghosts and postmaterial persons who visit during ADCs?* Visitations by ghosts are often described as feeling scary or sad, accompanied by physical coldness, and continuing for a long time. ADCs, on the other hand, are usually briefer and accompanied by feelings of peace, love, and joy.

Sometimes, however, earthly perceptions of which is occurring may not be so clear. Helen shared an example of this with me:

> "For three months after my son-in-law passed over in the war, there was an eerie sense of cold about the house. I heard heavy footsteps outside my bedroom window and encountered many sleepless nights due to being poked and pulled at. I knew deep inside who it could be, but chose to ignore it and prayed that tonight would be the night that I would get some rest. This was not to be and finally I had enough. I looked at his photo with tears streaming down my face and said to him, 'Okay, baby, I know there's something wrong and I will find someone who can help so you can be at peace.'
>
> As soon as I said that, the room felt suddenly warmer and brighter and a peace came over me that I can't really explain. He had passed over so quickly and tragically that he had unresolved issues and hadn't accepted his physical death. He only wanted somebody to help him. If I wasn't so keen on denying his presence, I could've helped him sooner. I found a medium to help send him into the Light. Those incidents never occurred again."

In the *Sightings* documentary, Kerry Gaynor – an investigator at the UCLA paranormal research lab – said that seeing ghosts has been reported in all cultures since the beginning of time. He stated, "Research of photographic evidence has produced many hoaxes, but a handful of pictures defy explanation." Some of Gaynor's photos were featured in *Popular Photography*, the only alleged ghost pictures ever presented in that respected magazine at that time.

An NBC broadcast reported on "The Stately Ghosts of England." Professional photographers set up infrared movie cameras in a castle with a history of ghost sightings. Captured on film was a shaft of light clearly emerging from one door, traveling down a short hallway, and entering another door. One researcher stated, "All the lighting conditions were controlled, windows were blacked out, there was no possibility of moonlight or car headlights coming through. When we saw the stuff later, there was a shaft of light which to me is completely unexplainable." Decades later, this paranormal phenomenon is still unexplained. (8)

Spiritually Transformative Experiences

Spiritually transformative experiences (STE) impart a deeper knowing that you, and everyone else, are eternal and integral parts of life. Synonyms for the verb form of 'have a STE' include: *see the light, awaken to the greater reality, see the big picture of life,* and *become enlightened.*

Catalysts for STEs can vary greatly and include: NDE, ADC, OBE, birth of a child, meditation, prayer, chanting, bodily death of a loved one, and shared crossing experience. Other 'triggering events' for STEs are seeing beautiful nature scenes, learning the collective afterlife evidence, love-based religious / spiritual teachings, prudent use of consciousness-altering plants, soul-engaging music, and exposure to actual or potential violence.

Other persons describe activation of higher energy centers via deep relaxation / hypnosis sessions, transformative audio products, evidential reading from a medium, and deeply loving relationships. From my experiences working with many people, I would add coming to earth as an 'old' or advanced soul, and having enlightened role models and teachers. [F]

In short, as the saying goes, when the student is ready, the teacher will appear. That is, *most any stimulus can be the final piece of the puzzle that awakens you to your timeless nature.* The most inspiring examples I've seen involve STEs after the bodily death of a loved one.

I have worked with many grieving people over the last four decades, and intensively with bereaved parents over the last seven years. Understandably, most parents are initially devastated when their child transitions to the next phase of life. Some remain enmired – for many years, or the rest of their time on earth – in deep grief and lower-energy emotions of anger, blame, guilt, hopelessness, etc. Parents sometimes divorce, and / or become addicted to drugs and alcohol. Some choose to pass on by suicide because of the pain and desire to be with their child.

No one could fairly blame or judge any of this until walking a mile in their shoes.

However, some parents seek a higher road. *They choose to find the silver linings and blessings in this seeming tragedy.* They focus on the potential benefits – to themselves and others – of ***a grief-induced spiritually transformative experience.***

It's been a sacred privilege to assist this *miraculous process of transmutation* in parents. Instead of primarily identifying themselves as bereaved parents, they journey toward becoming *shining light parents.* Moment by moment, they reach for the highest feeling thoughts possible. A particularly powerful focus is that *their children are now* living in a realm where peace, joy, love, and light predominate. These parents strive to honor their children and create more meaning by shining more brightly and serving others.

Jeff and Lynn Hollahan, whose son Devon changed worlds in 2009, are great examples of this. He is a Helping Parents Heal board member and they both are Caring Listeners for that organization. Jeff spontaneously said during our conversation about becoming a shining light parent: 'When you find a fork in the road, go up.' This Yoga Berra-like saying speaks volumes. They are as enlightened, loving, and serving as anyone I know. Very impressive.

Many of these parents believe there is a rhyme and reason in the timing of their child's graduation from earth school. They seriously consider that pre-birth planning may have been involved for good reasons they may not understand now, but will someday.

Many shining light parents have found they can perceive their children more frequently and clearly by focusing on higher energies and emotions. This makes sense: afterlife realms usually involve greater awareness of peace, joy, love, and light. By choosing those ways of being, parents *can tune-in to a similar wavelength* and better detect their child's presence. [G]

> ***If bereaved parents can use such deep tragedy as a spring board to a spiritually transformative experience, nearly everyone can.***

The potential benefits of STEs for many people and our planet are invaluable. Anne shared her new perspective on what is often a very sad anniversary …

> "I just finished reading your book and it is amazing. Using the new words I learned from you, my husband graduated from earth-school one year ago today. Your book has given me a new peace and much more hopeful outlook. Thanks to you, I'm very confident that he will be the first person I'll see when I go to the next phase of life."

Electronic Device Phenomena

This term refers to reports of *alterations in electronic device functioning* purportedly caused by postmaterial persons. Variations of this fairly common phenomenon include: lights flickering, garage door opening, TV or radio turning on / off, and altered audio-video recordings.

After my patient Ted transitioned from earth, his widow Marilyn shared the following event. On the one-year anniversary of his passing, several family members visited Ted's grave site. Their son videotaped the monument, fresh flowers, and surrounding trees. He also filmed a sparrow that hopped around on the monument for most of the visit. One of them remarked that perhaps Ted was providing a sign through the bird. Later, they excitedly showed the recording to other family members. There was the monument, flowers, and trees – *but no sparrow.* That made more sense when they learned that 'spirits' can be difficult to capture on conventional film.

Multiple electronic aberrations occurred during the filming of my *Soul Proof* documentary film:

- Equipment malfunctions occurred as people we interviewed talked about their ADCs. The film crew could find no reason for these and we couldn't continue for over an hour.

- The equipment *resumed working immediately* after a spiritualist minister told 'spirits' that their presence was noted, and asked them to please not interfere with filming.

- Videographers said batteries needed replaced *much more often* than ever before.

The fields of *Electronic Voice Projection* (EVP) and *Instrumental Transcommunication* (ITC) describe, respectively, capturing audio and video images of postmaterial persons. Common electronic devices – tape recorders, video cameras, and computers – have allegedly captured sounds and images from postmaterial persons. Pioneers in these fields include:

- Konstantin Raudive, PhD, a student of Carl Jung, MD and author of *Breakthrough: An Amazing Experiment in Electronic Communication with the Dead*
- Ernst Senkowski, professor of physics and electrical engineering, who wrote *Instrumentelle Transkommunikation*
- Mark Macy, a journalist who authored *Miracles in the Storm*
- Tom and Lisa Butler, authors of *There is No Death and There Are No Dead*
- Dan Drasin, producer and director of the "Calling Earth" documentary
- Alexander McRae, engineer and ITC researcher

Attorney Sidney L. Freeman, author of *Life After Death: A Survey of the Cumulative Evidence,* conducted a thorough search of the existing information as would a trial lawyer. Of EVP research, he stated:

> "The most successful results were obtained with Dr. Konstantin Raudive, a Latvian psychologist. In the presence of guests, Dr. Raudive would record questions he asked aloud. After the questions, he paused

> and waited to hear answers. No answers were heard – either by him or the guests. But, miraculously, when the tapes were played back, answers were recorded on the tapes. Answers from whom? From his relatives and friends who had graduated from the earthly plane. To avoid any charge of trickery, fresh, sealed, blank tapes were used and inserted by many different observers. A total of 60,000 such voices were recorded during the period of experimentations. The publisher, *Taplinger Publishing Company* of New York City, verified the facts by many different scientists before releasing Raudives' book for publication." (13)

Frankly, I have the least exposure to and knowledge about this topic than any others I present. My impression, based on this limited data, is that the methods and purported results range from (1) clearly fraudulent to (2) possibly valid, but needing more scientific research.

The audio recordings I've heard are largely unintelligible and could easily be attributed to *auditory pareidolia* (interpreting random sounds as voices) or *apophenia* (perceiving patterns in random information). In addition, highly sensitive electronic equipment captures a lot of background noise that affects the quality of audio and video recordings. The video images I've seen were sometimes obtained beforehand and could have been altered.

A growing body of university-based research indicates that ultra-sensitive technology might someday be used to accurately and reliably detect the presence of postmaterial persons. Results of replicated and controlled experiments published by Gary E. Schwartz, PhD illustrates the promise for future 'spirit' communication. (9 - 12) I will describe his work further in the Scientific Research category.

For additional information about EVP and ITC, visit the Afterlife Research and Education Institute at AfterLifeInstitute.org.

Other Types of Firsthand Experiences

Extrasensory perceptions, although temporary and not verifiable, can be very impactful. *Just one otherworldly glimpse* can open one's mind to the reality of life after bodily death.

I have received many heartwarming emails and letters from people around the world who report personal perceptions of their postmaterial loved ones. Those firsthand experiences filled them with comfort, hope, and enthusiasm. They send photos, audio-video recordings, and other evidence of what they consider to be signs from 'deceased' loved ones.

However, as a serious researcher of afterlife evidence, I cannot verify the accuracy of their reports. I may personally believe them, but there is no objective data for these often nebulous images. I will share three extrasensory perceptions that I personally experienced and thus know are legitimate.

At a holistic health retreat in 1996, I walked toward the ocean and clearly saw two people swimming and then standing in the water. As I waded in, I saw a tall male with dark hair and a shorter female bobbing and diving under the water. As I approached more closely, the female waved and I recognized her as my good friend Elaine.

I wondered who the man was since her husband was shorter and had white hair. I couldn't see him and figured he was holding his breath under the water. When I reached Elaine, I looked around and asked, "Where's that guy?" She looked at me like I was crazy and said, "What guy? I've been out here by myself for twenty minutes." I described the fellow I had seen as clearly as I had seen her. She replied, "Maybe you saw one of my angels or guides?" Maybe.

As mentioned, I assisted with many 'Code 4' resuscitations while working in hospitals in the 1970s. In those days, dying patients seldom received attention to their emotional and spiritual needs. I was in theology school and reading books by Drs. Elisabeth Kubler Ross, Herman Feifel, and other pioneers in the emerging field of thanatology. As such, I was aware of this need and wasn't afraid of appearing kooky. While working with dying patients, I spoke directly into their ears, reassured them that everything possible was being done, and encouraged them to not be afraid. On several occasions, I saw ***a faint white light emanate from the patient's chest just before the time of death was called.***

I experienced what I considered to be the grace and beauty of an angel's visit in 1993 while completing my first book *Radiant Wellness.* While writing early one morning, I looked for a quote from the *Bible* but couldn't find it despite searching my *Concordance.* Then I suddenly felt ecstatic for no apparent reason and heard a slight rustling sound. Through my peripheral vision, I saw a white gauzy form – like the fine lacework of a wedding dress. As I turned to see it more clearly, that image was gone or, more likely, I just couldn't see it any longer.

I felt energized and interpreted this as a sign that my writing was in alignment with my soul's missions. ***Immediately afterwards***, I opened the *Bible* to the exact page I needed and my eyes went directly to the verses I sought: "What is humankind, that thou art mindful of them? … Thou made them a little lower than the angels; you crowned them with glory and honor." (Hebrews 2: 6 - 7)

Consciousness-altering plants or *entheogens* have facilitated perceptions of *nonordinary states of reality* – including life after death – for many people. Sharing the same root word with enthusiasm, *entheogen refers to bringing God within*. Different states of awareness while under the influence of, for example, peyote, mushrooms, and ayahuasca may engender perceptions similar to those during ADCs, OBEs, and NDEs. Religious and mystical practices in various cultures have gainfully used sacred botanical preparations to heighten awareness.

I don't recommend this path because of the potential pitfalls. Rather, I encourage meditation, prayer, yoga, centering practices, optimal nutrition, and other safe and time-tested methods that provide impressive results. But entheogens have worked well for some people who use them under appropriate and well-supervised conditions.

Common sense knowing is another indication that life continues after bodily death. This was beautifully stated in

Go Toward the Light by Chris Oyler. She described the moments after her nine-year-old son Ben passed on after contracting AIDS from a blood transfusion: "The room was full of Ben. He was all around us everywhere. Warm and loving. He was lingering for a moment to say good-bye. To tell us not to worry, that there wasn't anything to be afraid of, and never was … And you know that all that energy and love cannot just vanish without a trace." (14)

The 'Swiss watch analogy' is a common sense argument for the existence of a wise Higher Power and, thus, a good and just outcome that includes life after death. Following the logic of this *intelligent design argument*, imagine that you found an expensive Swiss watch on the ground. Would you conclude that the watch formed randomly and just fell out of the sky? Or might you deduce that *an organized intelligence* – a master watchmaker – created the timepiece that someone lost?

Similarly, consider the awesome complexity, evident on both micro and macro scales, in the human body and nature. An equally magnificent Creative Force of life is implied. Might this Infinite Intelligence include the continuation of consciousness after the earthly form dies?

As Benjamin Franklin put it: "When I see nothing annihilated and not a drop of water wasted, I cannot suspect the annihilation of souls, or believe that God will suffer the daily waste of millions of minds readymade that now exist, and put Himself to the continual trouble of making new ones. Thus, finding myself to exist in the world, I believe I shall, in some shape or other, always exist; and, with all the inconveniences human life is liable to, I shall not object to a new edition of mine, hoping, however, that the mistakes of the last may be corrected." (15)

Experiencing unity consciousness is another indication of your continuing oneness with all life. While driving over a long bridge years ago, I enjoyed a cherished moment of this. Glancing up, I saw a flock of geese flying in front of a fading sunset. Then I looked over to see the river and its snowy banks. *The entire scene seemed so familiar*, as if I had somehow helped design it. I immediately felt a deep sense of peace and unity with all of life.

Perhaps you've had at least one such moment. As one grows in unity consciousness, even fleeting and ordinary experiences can remind the observer that there is more to life than this brief earthly journey.

Ken Wilber, author of *No Boundary*, put it this way: "In unity consciousness, in no boundary awareness, the sense of self expands to totally include everything once thought to be not self." (16)

Centering practices to quiet the brain and perceive more of life include prayer, meditation, yoga, service to others, optimal self-care, time with loved ones, gardening, chanting, breathing exercises, and drumming. For some, the mind is most relaxed by playing with pets, spending time with elders, spiritual studies, sewing, exercising, bodywork, and energy movements like tai chi and qi gong. Other ways to – as Fritz Perls PhD said – 'lose your mind and come to your senses' include experiential seminars, hot baths, lovemaking, deep relaxation, shamanic trance work, and sacred dance.

The brain is an amazing organ but, as discussed, senses only a tiny fraction of reality. Centering practices allow you to be still and consider that life may be more enduring and safer than we can fathom.

In summary, firsthand experience evidence can be very impressive. However, *sometimes sensing is not believing*. Some people doubt their perceptions as time goes by and memories fade. Over time, what appeared to be very real experiences may seem more like daydreams or the imagination. To better remember and value your firsthand experiences that point to survival of life after death, I recommend:

- Write a detailed description of your experience as soon as possible.
- Discuss it with trusted family and friends.
- Learn evidence that supports the possible validity of your perceptions.
- Consider how you can help others with your newfound hope and vitality. Doing this further internalizes your glimpse of the field of all possibilities.

As I will discuss in Category 2, *evidence from clinical studies* has convinced many people that life continues after bodily death. Learning this evidence isn't a dry academic exercise; it's essential for living fully during your earthly experience. Here's how sixteen-year-old Tom put it:

> "Your book changed my life spiritually. I now feel happier about myself. You helped me put what my subconscious was feeling into conscious thinking. *I really am an eternal soul.* Thanks to you, I now realize this. This may sound like a small thing but, to me, it is just the beginning."

As Dave shares below, knowing this information can literally be the difference between continuing to live on earth versus choosing death of the human form …

> "I've been suicidal for about a year, bad, every day. Your articles are amazing. They really helped me a lot. I'm very grateful for you. What a great service you provide for humanity. My spiritual awakening has been brutal and I didn't know if I could stay on this planet much longer. I came across your work today. Words cannot express. You are saving so many like me, I am positive of that. Thank you again so much."

Category 2

Evidence from Clinical Studies

Clinical studies include data collected and analyzed by a university professor, physician, and / or psychologist in a professional office or hospital.

Subcategories include: *near-death experiences, past life memories and regressions, perinatal experiences, life between lives sessions, shared crossings, terminal lucidity cases,* and *deathbed visions.*

Near-Death Experiences

When I was nine years old, my Uncle Cliff's car collided with a semi. His body nearly died from severe multiple injuries and he was in the hospital for a long time. When he finally came home, he was pale, thin, missing teeth, and couldn't walk. From his hospital bed in the family living room, he spoke through a wired jaw about his experience while almost dead. He described walking in a meadow of lush green grass, hearing beautiful music, and seeing a figure of light he identified as Jesus. With a far-away look, he spoke of everything being more brilliant and colorful than usual. Uncle Cliff felt so peaceful that, except for missing his family, he didn't care if he came back. He no longer feared bodily death.

That was the first time I heard of near-death experiences (NDEs). It made a big impression on me and increased my openness to similar reports by patients I worked with in hospitals. Several of them told me about their NDE after being resuscitated. They were very excited about seeing the Light and feeling unfathomable love and understanding. After that, I made a point of visiting people who had been successfully resuscitated. I gently inquired: 'Do you remember anything while you were unconscious?' Their reports were fascinating.

Many documented NDEs provide impressive clinical evidence for the continuation of life beyond the grave. 'Documented NDE' means that, while clinically dead, people were aware of events occurring in the room and surrounding areas. Keep in mind that these nearly deceased patients often arrived at the hospital in comatose conditions, and their eyes were closed during the resuscitative procedures. Nonetheless, they accurately perceived events and described details about them to hospital staff.

NDEs have been reported independently and similarly across time in various cultures. As described in *The Tibetan Book of the Dead, The Egyptian Book of the Dead,* and *The Aztec Song of the Dead*, NDEs were first reported thousands of years ago. Studies of diverse age groups in other cultures show the same patterns or universality of NDE reports. Much NDE research exists thanks to pioneers such as Drs. Raymond Moody, Ken Ring, Bruce Greyson, Melvin Morse, Stan Grof, Pim von Lommel, Michael Sabom, George Ritchie, and others.

According to Ken Ring, PhD, professor emeritus at the University of Connecticut, clinical research has confirmed *nearly ten thousand documented NDE cases.* There are so many of these validated cases that they are collectively known as *tennis shoe stories.* This term arose from actual cases in which clinically dead persons saw objects like an old tennis shoe on top of the hospital or window ledge. (17)

Brian Weiss, MD, in his book *Messages from the Masters,* described a number of NDEs with verifiable aspects. One woman suffered massive head trauma from a severe auto accident and was very near death. As the doctor spoke with the family about the quite probable fatal outcome, the patient floated out of her body. She found her family even though they were far from where the medical team was working on her body. Upon overhearing the conversation, she tried to communicate to them that *she wasn't really dead.* After her recovery, she accurately repeated the conversation between the surgeon and her family.

Said Dr. Weiss, "I have heard these and other stories of clinical accounts of patients with near-death and out-of-body experiences from so many physicians that I cannot explain them away on medical or physiological grounds." (18)

Further validation that NDEs are not imaginary or anoxia-induced are provided by ***'surprise meetings'.*** These involve encounters during the NDE with people the survivor didn't know had died. In *The Light Beyond,* Dr. Moody told of a woman who was very ill at the same time her sister was near death on a different floor of the same hospital. During her NDE, the woman watched the resuscitative efforts on her body from above. To her surprise, she met her sister and they enjoyed a great conversation until the sister began moving away. The woman stated, "I tried to go with her, but she kept telling me to stay where I was. 'It's not your time,' she said … Then she just began to recede off into the distance through a tunnel while I was left there alone. When I awoke, I told the doctor that my sister had died. He denied it, but at my insistence, he had a nurse check on it. She had in fact died, just as I knew she did." (19)

Documented cases involving children, who should have less knowledge about consciousness topics, are *especially impressive.* In *Closer to the Light,* Melvin Morse, MD and Paul Perry tell of an eight-year-old boy who fell from a bridge and hit his head on a rock in the water. After floating face down for at least five minutes, he was pulled from the water by a policeman. The boy had stopped breathing and didn't have a pulse. After performing CPR for thirty minutes, the policeman declared him dead. Even so, a helicopter emergency team started resuscitation and rushed him to the hospital. The boy didn't regain consciousness until two days later when he accurately described his rescue and resuscitation in great detail. He knew all of this, he said, because he had been watching the whole time from outside his body. (20)

Even more impressive are ***documented NDEs involving blind people – some of whom have been blind since birth.*** NDE experts consider these cases to be the most difficult to explain unless consciousness indeed exists independently of the brain. In the foreword of *Mindsight* by Ken Ring, PhD and Sharon Cooper, PhD, researcher Charles T. Tart, PhD stated: "The authors of this book have practiced essential science, real science. They have looked at the facts about NDEs, particularly NDEs among the blind, and provided us with extremely stimulating and thought-provoking material that we must take into account in coming to terms with reality ... these facts argue strongly that there is some very real sense in which we are 'spiritual' beings, not just material beings." (21)

Dr. Ring added that a panel of vision specialists had no medical explanations to explain accurate perceptions of blind people while clinically dead. (22)

In *Books of the Dead*, Stan Grof, MD discussed: "... reported cases where individuals, who were blind because of medically confirmed organic damage to their optical system, could at the time of clinical death see the environment." He continued, "Occurrences of this kind, unlike most of the other aspects of near-death phenomena, can be subjected to objective verification. They thus represent the most convincing proof that what happens in near-death experiences is more than the hallucinatory phantasmagoria of physiologically impaired brains." (23)

For more than thirty years, Dutch cardiologist Pim van Lommel, MD, author of *Consciousness Beyond Life: The Science of the Near-Death Experience*, studied NDEs in patients who survived cardiac arrest. In 2001, he and fellow researchers published a study in the prestigious medical journal *The Lancet*. Lommel stated that the NDE is an authentic experience that cannot be attributed to imagination, psychosis, or oxygen deprivation. (24)

Neurosurgeon Eben Alexander, MD, author of *Proof of Heaven,* had an NDE after a severe case of bacterial meningitis.

This infection should have resulted in death or at least permanent and profound brain damage. During a weeklong coma, Dr. Alexander came to understand deep truths about the nature of reality and consciousness. Based on his professional and personal experiences, Alexander believes the brain does not create consciousness. Rather, he maintains that awareness is primal and survives death of the human body.

Past Life Memories and Past Life Regressions

The term *past life memory* describes *spontaneous recollections* of events in another time and place. These usually occur with children, but may be suddenly triggered in adults. *Past life regression* is a session using hypnosis in which clients may recall experiences in another time and place.

A past life memory with no evidentiary aspects happened when our daughter was four years old. After I read her a bedtime story, she drifted off to sleep and murmured: "I remember before I came to be with you. The sun always shined, it never rained, and I always wore pretty dresses. And, oh yes, Greg was there too!" (Greg was a pre-school buddy with whom there was an immediate mutual attraction.) Then she stopped talking. I waited, then quietly prompted her: "Tell me more, what else do you remember?" She awakened and said, "Oh, I must have been dreaming."

Some past life memories contain impressive validation features that strengthen the case for them being more than vivid imagination. One such case was described in the book *Across Time and Death* by Jenny Cockell. As a child, Jenny had vivid, recurrent dreams of dying from a fever and leaving behind eight young children. She awakened from these dreams sobbing and feeling terribly sad and guilty about leaving them. While very young, Jenny drew maps and scenes of a small Irish village and continued to do so over the years.

As an adult, she traced her former identity to Mary Sutton, who had indeed died from a fever and had eight children. Jenny traveled to Ireland and had emotional reunions with Mary's now grown children. They verified that Jenny knew details only their mother could have known. After this contact with her children, Jenny no longer suffered from recurrent dreams, guilt, and sadness. (25)

Carol Bowman, MA, author of *Children's Past Lives,* was an early researcher in this field. She related a case from England as reported by Peter and Mary Harrison in *The Children That Time Forgot*: "Desmond had been playing with his toy cars on the floor when he told his mother, without any prompting, 'You know, Mummy, I went to Aunty Ruth before I came to you, but I didn't stay there very long.' His mother was stunned to hear her three-and a-half-year old say this. Her sister-in-law, Ruth, had given birth to a stillborn son ten years before. But the family had a pact to never speak of it because it had been so traumatic for her. Desmond could never have overheard anyone discuss it." Describing his time in Ruth's womb, Desmond said, "One time I went to sleep, but when I woke up again I wasn't with Aunty Ruth anymore." (26)

As mentioned, the term ***past life regression describes hypnosis-assisted recall of possible experiences in other times and places.***

Joel Whitton, MD, PhD, was a professor of psychiatry at the University of Toronto Medical School and co-author with Joe Fisher of *Life Between Life*. They related Whitton's clinical work with a client named Harold who, when hypnotized, described a former life as a Viking raider. Although Harold had never studied a foreign language, he spoke comfortably and confidently in a strange tongue that experts identified as ancient Norse.

Working independently, linguists who spoke Icelandic and Norwegian identified and translated some of these words. Several other words seemed to have a Russian, Serbian or Slavic derivation. One language expert stated, "It would be appropriate for a Viking to speak a language which contained words and phrases of other tongues in that period. I would say this could fit the language pattern of the roving Viking."

During another past life recollection, Harold wrote what looked like scribbles. The alphabet he used was identified by researchers as a long-extinct script used in Mesopotamia. That language bears no relation to modern Iranian and hasn't been spoken for more than 1300 years. Of Harold's past-life regression experiences, Dr. Whitton stated, "To me, the case remains one of the most convincing arguments I've seen for evidence of reincarnation." (27)

Dr. Weiss has received *thousands* of phone calls and letters from psychiatrists, psychologists, and other therapists who have done past life regressions for up to twenty years. He stated, "The letters describe detailed accounts of past-life recall, of patients recalling names, dates, and details of lifetimes in other cities, countries or continents. Some patients have found their 'old' names in the official records of places they have never even heard of, let alone visited, in this lifetime. Some have found their own tombstones." (28)

Clinical evidence for the validity of past life memories and regressions includes: *child prodigies, familiarity, xenoglossy, curative evidence, similarities between lives, and documented past life cases.*

Child prodigies have demonstrated amazing abilities in music, mathematics, and other fields. Some have displayed virtuoso musical abilities despite being very young and having little or no practice with that instrument. Mozart, for example, composed a concerto at age four.

In *How to Know God*, Deepak Chopra, MD described the most famous musical prodigy of the present generation, Russian pianist Evgeny Kissin. His mother vividly recalls that her one-year-old hummed Bach melodies in perfect pitch. "And as soon as Evgeny could toddle, he made his way to the family piano and began to pick out the same Bach exercises that he had heard his older sister practicing. These were just the first signs exhibited by a child prodigy who was composing music at six and performing both Chopin piano concertos in a single concert at age thirteen—a prodigious feat even for an accomplished virtuoso."

Chopra added, "People who spend time with geniuses and prodigies often find them unearthly, somehow preternatural, as if a very old soul has been confined to a new body and yet brings in experience far beyond what that body could have known. It is easy to credit that some kind of former life is casting its influence on the present. Speaking of his own experience, one musical prodigy stated, 'It is as if I am playing from outside my own consciousness. The music comes through me. I am the conduit, not the source.'" (29)

Familiarity is another puzzling occurrence unless the field of all possibilities can indeed be experienced from other observation points. Familiarity involves having detailed knowledge of a particular historical period, place, or person that one has never studied, visited, or met. For example, upon arriving at a city for the first time, some people know specific directions and locations of landmarks.

Even more common is meeting someone for the first time and having a strong sense of knowing each other. This may partially account for the instant fondness or dislike felt toward new acquaintances. Familiarity has been reported many times during hypnotic past life regressions and spontaneous past life memories.

Dr. Weiss described a case involving familiarity as well as a possible cause-and-effect explanation of health problems. Diane, a registered nurse, was unmarried and had been looking without success for a soulmate relationship. During a past-life regression with Weiss, she recalled an earlier lifetime as a pioneer woman who hid with her baby from Indians. To keep the baby quiet, she covered his mouth with her hand. The baby, who had a crescent-shaped birthmark beneath his right shoulder, died as she accidentally asphyxiated him.

Several months after this regression, Diane treated a man with asthma at her hospital job. She nearly fainted when, while listening to his lungs, she saw a crescent-shaped birthmark below his right shoulder. Both experienced an instant familiarity and connection that led to dating and a happy marriage. (30)

Xenoglossy is the phenomenon of being able to speak one or more languages fluently without any exposure to them in this present lifetime. In *Reincarnation: The Phoenix Fire Mystery*, authors Cranston and Head related the story of Dr. Marshall McDuffie, a prominent New York physician, and his wife Wilhelmina whose: " ... twin baby boys were found to be conversing among themselves in some unknown vernacular. The children were eventually taken to the foreign language department of Columbia University, but none of the professors present could identify their speech. However, a professor of ancient languages happened to pass by and was amazed to discover that the babies were speaking Aramaic, a language current at the time of Christ." (31)

Frederick Lenz, PhD, author of *Lifetimes: True Accounts of Reincarnation*, described a mother's account of her daughter's nighttime xenoglossy. The parents were awakened by the sound of a strange voice coming from the bedroom of their six-year old daughter. They found her talking in her sleep and speaking rapidly in French. The mother stated, "My daughter is six and has never been outside this country and has never been exposed to anyone who speaks French." When this happened several nights in a row, the parents taped the conversation and took it to a local French teacher. "She listened to it and told us that the little girl (our daughter) on the tape was looking for her mother, who she had been separated from when her village was attacked by the Germans. She said the little girl seemed to be lost and, judging from her tone of voice, was very distressed. It is my feeling that our daughter lived before in a village in France and probably died in one of the world wars." (32)

Curative evidence for living in other times and places includes healing of emotional and physical disorders after a past life memory or regression. The existence of unexplainable phobias, for example, fear of guillotines in the 21st century, suggests that unresolved traumas may have carried over from past lives. Cures of these difficult disorders are especially impressive since they are often spontaneous and occur after numerous orthodox approaches have failed. These therapeutic recoveries are often total and lasting.

Margie, a sixty-five-year-old woman who suffered with chronic and severe back pain, was referred to me for a past life regression by her integrative medical doctor. Margie had literally tried everything: chiropractic, physical therapy, acupuncture, hypnosis for pain management, injections, medications, massage, and energy healing. But none of these approaches diminished her pain.

Despite being deeply relaxed during our past life regression session, Margie became quite agitated as she described her life during medieval times as a servant girl to an evil and powerful man. Margie saw herself being raped and abused by this man over a period of several years. She couldn't escape and could not bear to live like that. While crying and trembling, she described trying to stab him so he wouldn't hurt her anymore. Her frail attempt was thwarted and the man stabbed her in the back several times directly over the area where her chronic pain was. After this cathartic session, Margie reported feeling 75% better. Her improvement increased over time and persisted two years later when I last heard from her.

Hans Holzer, PhD described Israeli bio-energetic healer Ze'ev Kolman's abilities to know and use past life information. Said Holzer, "Increasing numbers of doctors take quite seriously symptoms caused by situations in previous lives that are unknown to the sufferer, because there are positive results to back them up. When the patient understands the origin of the affliction, it appears that the matter is solved." (33)

Michael Newton, PhD, founder of *Life Between Lives* therapy, was a traditional psychologist for many years. He resisted requests for past life regressions until he worked with a man who suffered with severe pain. Dr. Newton stated, "This client complained of a lifetime of chronic pain on his right side. I eventually uncovered his former life as a World War I soldier who was killed by a bayonet in France, and we were able to eliminate the pain altogether ... I came to appreciate just how therapeutically important the link is between the bodies and events of our former lives and who we are today." (34)

Similarities between lives were most thoroughly investigated by Ian Stevenson, MD, who headed the department of psychiatry at the University of Virginia. He spent most of his sixty-year career perfecting methods for verifying past life memories of children. Dr. Stevenson's books include *Children Who Remember Previous Lives, Twenty Cases Suggestive of Reincarnation, Reincarnation and Biology,* and *Where Reincarnation and Biology Intersect.* In the latter book, a two-volume set with 2,268 pages, Dr. Stevenson showed pictures of people in present and purported past lives. Physical resemblances of present-day birth marks or deformities associated with past life injuries are striking.

Walter Semkiw, MD also extensively researched the topic of similarities between lives. He holds that, from lifetime to lifetime, people tend to exhibit similar physical characteristics and persistent personality traits. Many of the physical resemblances Semkiw shows are eerily similar. In addition, he identifies similar modes of expression such as writing styles. Symbols and synchronistic events that reflect important features of a person's past lives, he claims, are often found in a current lifetime. Dr. Semkiw used public records and historical archives to document these parallel features. His book *Return of the Revolutionaries* shows numerous pictures of people as they look now and as they did in alleged past lives.

Documented past life memory cases have been thoroughly investigated at the Division of Perceptual Studies at the University of Virginia School of Medicine. [H] This research was led by Dr. Stevenson until his passing in 2007. Jim Tucker, MD, author of *Life Before Life* and *Return to Life*, continued Dr. Stevenson's and other research in this area.

Dr. Stevenson and his staff compiled over 3,000 cases from Asia, Europe, Africa and North America. Nearly 900 of these were stringently verified and 35 percent of the people involved had birthmarks or birth defects that matched injuries from previous lives. Eighteen of these cases involved two or more matching birthmarks. Stevenson calculated the chances that *two matching sets of birthmarks – from a purported past life and the present one* – would occur randomly were only 1 in

25,600. ***The odds against this happening by chance eighteen times are astronomical.***

Stevenson's stringent standards of research relied heavily on private and repeated interviews over time. He wrote a clinical textbook for psychiatrists based on methods used by attorneys to reconstruct past events as accurately as possible. Dr. Stevenson and his team investigated children who remembered possible past lives and their family members. Then they traveled to the town where the child purportedly lived before and interviewed people there. Given the exacting methods of these professional researchers, it was virtually impossible for anyone – especially third-world villagers – to conceal a hoax.

Here are three examples of Stevenson's cases:

- Parmod, a 3 ½ year-old boy from India, remembered owning a soda and bakery store in another town. Upon arriving in that town, he led his family directly to the shop. He knew how to repair a complex soda machine that had been intentionally disconnected to test his memory.

- Michael, a 3-year-old from Texas, remembered exact details of a fatal auto accident in his previous life. His recollection was that of being his mother's high school boyfriend who died just as Michael described.

- At just 1 ½ years of age, Sukla of India cradled a toy and said it was her daughter Minu. During the next several years, she remembered more details of her past life so

> her family took her to that village. Sukla directed them to her former home and enjoyed a reunion with Minu whose mother had died when she was a baby.

Jenny Wade, PhD, author of *Changes of Mind*, stated that Stevenson's research has withstood every serious challenge to date because of the impressive documentation and rigorous scientific methods used. Especially convincing, said Dr. Wade, is the high incidence of birthmarks and deformities in this life that correspond to injuries in an alleged former one. (35)

Peri-Natal Experiences

Perinatal experiences are particularly fascinating because they point to ***awareness that predates human birth***. The term 'perinatal' refers to the time period just before, during and after birth. Research on awareness during this timeframe suggests that *a wise and objective consciousness resides within the developing and newborn baby.*

In their book *Mindsight*, Ring and Cooper reviewed perinatal research and noted an emerging picture of *a dual nature of human consciousness.* The ***brain-based consciousness*** develops as the fetus grows. In addition, however, a great deal of empirical evidence points to a ***transcendent source of consciousness*** that "predates physical life and survives bodily death." They found that the transcendent source of awareness is most apparent during NDEs, mystical states of consciousness, and perinatal experiences. But it is usually overshadowed by brain-based awareness that predominates perceptions during an earthly experience. (36)

A perinatal experience with evidential aspects was reported in *Babies Remember Birth* by David Chamberlain, PhD. He stated: "Jason, a three-and-a-half year-old boy, surprised his mother by saying that he remembered being born, that he had heard her crying and was doing everything he could to get out. It was 'tight,' he felt 'wet,' and felt something around his neck and throat. In addition something hurt his head and he remembered his face had been 'scratched up.' Jason's mother said she had 'never talked to him about the birth, never,' but the facts were correct. The umbilical cord was wrapped around his neck, he was monitored via an electrode on his scalp, and was pulled out by forceps."

Dr. Chamberlain hypnotically regressed ten mothers and their children who had not been told any details about their births. He concluded that their reports were remarkably consistent and "dovetailed at various points like one story told from two points of view." Validated details included instruments used, people present, time of day, and other specifics of the delivery. The timing of various events was also reported accurately during these independent interviews of mothers and children. Chamberlain said that, considering all the facts, "... objectively gathered birth memories appear to be genuine recollections of experience." (37)

Regarding perinatal experiences, Dr. Grof – author of *Beyond the Brain* – stated: "I have been able to confirm the accuracy of many such reports ... [Subjects] have been able to recognize specificities and anomalies of their fetal position, detailed mechanics of labor, the nature of obstetric interventions, and the particulars of postnatal care. The experience of a breech position, placenta previa, the umbilical cord twisted around the neck, castor oil applied during the birth process, the use of forceps, various manual maneuvers, different kinds of anesthesia, and specific resuscitation procedures are just a few examples of the phenomena observed." (38)

Another resource on this topic is the book *Coming from the Light* by Sarah Hinze. She presented over thirty personal stories from parents who described ***connections with their children before conception and during pregnancy***. Interestingly, *these prenatal communications also occurred among adoptive parents during the pre-adoption period.* This suggests several possibilities, for example, that there is a pre-birth transcendent connection between the developing baby and prospective parents – even non-biological ones.

Life Between Lives Sessions

As mentioned, Michael Newton, PhD was a traditional psychologist at the beginning of his career. However, he became open to new approaches after several of his hypnotized clients described glimpses of what they considered spiritual realms. Dr. Newton systematically explored client reports about this possibility.

Over time, his work mapped out what subjects experienced before human birth. His *Life Between Lives* approach used four-hour long and very deep hypnotic regressions to access the time before coming to earth. *Dr. Newton conducted this pioneering work for over twenty-five years before sharing his findings with the world.* He facilitated sessions with over

7,000 people during his thirty-five-year career. These clients came from around the world. However, regardless of their geographical location, there was a high degree of consistency about specific details. His books *Journey of Souls* and *Destiny of Souls* described these early findings.

Dr. Newton stated, "I was a skeptic before about the whole process of past life regression and working with life between lives. What convinced me it was real was *the consistency of my patients' reports* as they were telling me everything that had happened to them in their past life reports. It didn't matter whether someone came to me who was deeply religious or an atheist, or any philosophical persuasion in between. Once I had them in deep hypnosis, they all told me the same thing about the spirit world and about their life between lives." (39)

Ann Clark, PhD, RN is the author of *Healing from Great Loss,* and co-author of *Wisdom of Souls* and *Llewellyn's Little Book of Life between Lives.* A certified Life Between Lives facilitator, Dr. Clark is the former Director of Research for the Newton Institute. She stated: "To date, approximately 65,000 LBL sessions have been conducted worldwide in 48 countries and in 21 different languages. Findings about otherworldly realms have remained consistent with clients from different cultures, ethnicities, and religions. During sessions, individuals experience themselves as immortal souls. Further, they meet guides, departed loved ones, and wise beings who offer advice on soul lessons and life purpose." Interestingly, said Clark, clients report transformative outcomes that show striking similarities to those after NDEs. (40)

Shared Crossings

The term *shared crossing* describes *NDE-like experiences reported by those present at the time of another's bodily death.* That is, these are described by healthy people during the time period when another person passes on. Shared crossings usually occur when there is a close relationship between the dying person and family members, friends, or health care providers.

I first heard about this phenomenon in 1999 when Dr. Moody described what he called *empathic NDEs.* In his book *The Last Laugh,* he stated: "Dozens upon dozens of first-rate individuals have related to me that, as a loved one died, they themselves lifted out of their own bodies and accompanied their dying loved ones upward toward a beautiful and loving light. Others have said that, as they sat with their dying loved ones, they perceived deceased relatives coming to greet the one who was passing away. Lots of doctors and nurses have described to me how they perceived patients' spirits leaving their bodies at the point of death." (41)

William Peters, MA, MEd, MFT, founded and directs the *Shared Crossing Project.* Their website at SharedCrossing.com states: "A shared crossing refers to experiences that convey information pertaining to an impending death and / or to the perceived continuation of consciousness after bodily death. This information often provides comfort and support for the dying as well as for loved ones and caregivers throughout and after the dying process. Experiencers often report that they have received a gift or transmission crafted specifically for them."

My friend Lisa Sharpe Jones, CPA, wrote about her shared crossing experience:

> "My husband Ian had been very ill with cancer for seven years and was near death. I prayed to God and the angels that, when the time was right, they would take Ian quickly and painlessly. I drifted off to sleep and *awoke in a most breathtaking place* surrounded by gleaming white and gold open-air buildings under a brilliant blue sky with shimmering clouds. Souls hurriedly scurried from one place to another preparing a huge feast. The whole scene oozed a palpable sense of excitement. *An angel said, 'Lisa, we are preparing for the arrival of the Great Ian Sharpe. We have been preparing for a long time, and the time is near for his brilliant soul to come and join us!'* I had such a sense of euphoria and was caught up in the moment when trumpets sounded and then...
>
> I heard through the door 'Lisa, Lisa, wake up. We think Ian just passed away!' I jolted awake after sleeping for almost three hours. I wasn't sure how I would react when Ian died, but I didn't think it would feel so peaceful and filled with unconditional love. (I learned the next day that – at the same time and half-way across the country – my mother also had a dream about Ian who had come to say goodbye.)
>
> Later that morning, I was drying my hair, and suddenly Ian's voice was in my left ear, 'Oh my God, Lisa. I love you ... but it's so AWESOME here!' I was so startled that I dropped the blow dryer. This was the beginning

> of receiving clear messages from Ian and other beings for the past 17 years."

In *Fire in the Soul,* Joan Borysenko, PhD – cofounder of the Harvard Mind-Body clinic – related a beautiful experience that occurred at the moment of her mother's passing. Her mother had long been critical and cynical of Joan's impressive academic and professional accomplishments. Joan and her son Justin were present as her mom transitioned from earth. At that moment, the room was filled with light and both realized what Justin verbalized: "I feel like Grandma is holding the door to eternity open to give us a glimpse. Can you feel it? You must be so grateful to your mother. You know, she was a very great soul. And she embodied to take a role that was much smaller than the wisdom in her soul and she did it as a gift for you so that you'd have something to resist." (42)

You'll recall my perceptions of a faint white light emanating from the patient's chest just before the time of bodily death was called. Looking back, perhaps my empathy for those in transition enabled these sixth-sense experiences.

Terminal Lucidity Cases

Terminal lucidity refers to a return to mental clarity in a person with profound memory loss or mental disorder. This occurrence during the days or hours before bodily death has been noted in patients with severe Alzheimer's disease, stroke, psychosis, and mental disability. Terminal lucidity events have been reported for over 250 years by doctors across the world.

German biologist Michael Nahm, PhD stated: "The literature concerned with experiences of the dying contains numerous accounts reporting the sudden return of mental clarity shortly before death. These experiences can be described as Terminal Lucidity. The most peculiar cases concern patients suffering from mental disability including mental illness or dementia." (43)

In the *Journal of Nervous and Mental Disease*, Nahm and Bruce Greyson, MD stated that, out of 49 case studies of terminal lucidity, 84 percent occurred within a week of bodily death. In addition, 43 percent occurred on the final day of life on earth. They and other researchers also published a related article in the July 2012 *Archives of Gerontology and Geriatrics.*

Stafford Betty, PhD, professor at California State University, wrote a *Huffington Post* blog entitled *When Alzheimer's Victims Suddenly 'Perk Up' Just Before Death - What's Going On?* Of one case, Dr. Betty stated: "An elderly woman never speaks; no longer recognizes her loved ones when they come to visit and shows no expression. By the looks of her, she is a human vegetable. And she's been this way for over a year. Her brain's cerebral cortex and hippocampus, necessary for memory, thought, language, and normal consciousness, are severely shrunken. Her brain bears little resemblance to a healthy one."

He continued, "Yet something utterly astonishing is about to happen. As reported by both the nursing staff of her care unit and her family members: unexpectedly, she calls her daughter and thanks her for everything. She has a phone conversation with her grandchildren, exchanges kindness and warmth. She says farewell and shortly thereafter dies."

Using the term 'mind' to describe consciousness, Dr. Betty stated: "Conventional brain science has no explanation. It has long been assumed that as the brain goes, so goes the mind, for the brain is what gives rise to the mind. Could it be that the conventional wisdom is wrong? Is it possible that the mind's sudden and short-lived return to normalcy just before death is brought about, not by some inexplicable surge in brain functioning, but by the mind's distancing itself from the brain? What if the brain does not give rise to the mind, as commonly thought? What if the mind uses the brain as its organ?" (44)

Jesse Bering wrote an article *One Last Goodbye: The Strange Case of Terminal Lucidity* in a *Scientific American* blog: "A 92-year-old woman with advanced Alzheimer's disease, for instance, hadn't recognized her family for years, but the day before her death, she had a pleasantly bright conversation with them, recalling everyone's name. She was even aware of her own age and where she'd been living all this time."

Bering stated that Alexander Batthyany, PhD, professor of cognitive science at the University of Vienna, conducted the first large-scale study on terminal lucidity. Dr. Bethany sent detailed questionnaires to caregivers – mostly nurses and medical doctors – of Alzheimer's victims. One of his respondents described how she used to consider advanced Alzheimer's patients as 'human vegetables.' However, a single instance of seeing terminal lucidity changed her outlook completely: "Had you seen what I saw, you could understand that dementia can affect the soul, but not destroy it." (45)

Death Bed Visions

Deathbed visions have been studied at the Division of Perceptual Studies at the University of Virginia's School of Medicine. Their website states: "Deathbed visions are those visions or other experiences that a dying person may have in the minutes, hours or days before his or her death. Family members or hospital personnel may report that a dying person, previously weak or even comatose, suddenly revived, sat up, stared at a corner of the room and called out the name of a deceased loved one. In rarer cases, a bystander has had such a vision, either alone or simultaneously with the dying person." (46)

Only ten percent of patients are conscious just before bodily death, but estimates are that *more than fifty percent of these experience a deathbed vision.* That is a very high rate of occurrence.

On three different occasions while working in hospitals, an elderly female patient told me, 'I don't what it is, but there's something different about you.' ***Then they described seeing their 'deceased' husbands standing at the foot of the bed.*** *The telepathic messages from their husbands were very similar: 'I love you. Don't worry. We will see each other again soon.'* These women were quite ill, but still keen of mind and oriented. They were very excited about what they sensed, but concerned about what others would think. *Each woman passed on within 48 hours of sharing their experiences.*

In 2017, Stephen Wagner wrote a ThoughtCo.com article entitled *Deathbed Visions: Are Dying People Escorted to the*

Other Side by Loved Ones? He stated: "Close to the moment of death, apparitions of deceased friends and loved ones appear to escort the dying to the other side. Such deathbed visions are not just the stuff of stories and movies. They are, in fact, more common than you might think and are surprisingly similar across nationalities, religions and cultures. Instances of these unexplained visions have been recorded throughout history and stand as one of the most compelling proofs of life after death."

Wagner continued, "One of the first to examine the subject seriously was Sir William Barrett, a Professor of Physics at the Royal College of Science in Dublin. In 1926, he published a summation of his findings in a book titled *Deathbed Visions*. In the many cases he studied, he discovered some interesting aspects of the experience that are not easily explained. It was not uncommon for the dying people who saw these visions to identify friends and relatives who they thought were still living."

Wagner concluded, "But in each case, according to Barrett, it was later discovered that these people had actually died. (Remember that then, communication wasn't what it is today; it might have taken weeks or even months to learn that a friend or a loved one had died.) Barrett found it curious that children quite often expressed surprise that the 'angels' they saw in their dying moments did not have wings. If the deathbed vision is just a hallucination, wouldn't a child see an angel as most often depicted in art and literature – with large, white wings?" (47)

Marilyn Mendoza, PhD, is a clinical instructor in the psychiatry department at Tulane University Medical Center and author of *We Do Not Die Alone*. In her *Psychology Today* blog,

Deathbed Visions: Experiences of the Dying, she wrote: "A patient dying of cancer had been very restless throughout the night. In the early morning, she opened her eyes and stared fixedly into the corner of the room where no one was standing. She said, 'Mom, I'm so glad to see you.' She smiled. After saying this, the tension in the room from the family eased. After her comment, the patient died peacefully."

Dr. Mendoza described another case: "A 52-year-old woman was dying of a failed transplant. She was terrified of dying and often spoke about how she was never going to give into death. Two days before her death, she kept looking over my shoulder and laughing and smiling at someone standing behind me. There was no one there. I asked the patient who she was talking to and she told me her dead father. Then she said, 'OK, all right. It's OK, I'm not afraid.' She then died very peacefully, smiling."

Mendoza noted, "Mothers tend to be the most frequently appearing figure in deathbed visions. Many times, it is the mother who comes to retrieve her child, no matter how old that child may be. Perhaps it is true when they say that a mother's work is never done. Nurses have reported to me that when the dying start to call for their mothers that death is not far behind."

Dr. Mendoza said that *more than one family member may appear at the same time* during a death bed vision as in the following case: "An elderly woman kept talking to her mother and her brother. Both of whom were deceased. She carried on several conversations with them. She would smile and drift off to sleep. Finally, in a conversation with them she agreed that it was time to go home. She died peacefully."

Additionally, *postmaterial pets* sometimes arrive with family members to help the person whose human form is dying. Dr. Mendoza wrote: "A 67-year-old woman saw her husband who had died four years previously, with her 22-year-old deceased dog. She stated that her husband had taken her hand and along with the old dog told her he would show her the path to follow to be able to die peacefully." (48)

Regarding his experience with death bed visions, Melvin Morse, MD, author of *Parting Visions,* said he has heard such cases for over ten years from numerous nurses and medical doctors. Initially, these dedicated health care professionals were reticent to share what they've witnessed with patients just before bodily death. But the growing number of such reports and immediate peace for the patients strengthens the credibility.

Carla Wills-Brandon, MA, author of *One Last Hug Before I Go,* wrote: "The visitors in the visions were often times deceased relatives who came to offer support to the dying person. In some situations, the dying did not know these visitors were already dead. Many of the individuals who have these visions are not on medications and are very coherent ... There is one aspect of some deathbed visions that is most difficult to explain and lends the most credence to the idea that they are actual visitations of spirits from 'the other side.' On rare occasions, the spirit entities are seen not only by the dying patient, but also by the friends, relatives, and others in attendance." (49)

Veteran psychical researchers Karlis Osis, PhD and Erlendur Haraldsson, PhD, authors of *At the Hour of Death,* stated there is mounting scientific evidence for life after death. They conducted extensive interviews of over one thousand doctors and nurses who were present when dying patients reported death bed visions. Extensive computer analyses of their observations were made. The authors collated this compelling evidence that suggests life persists after death of the human form. They observed the following:

1. Although some dying people report seeing angels and other religious figures, the vast majority claim to see familiar people who had previously passed away.

2. Very often, the friends and relatives seen in these visions express directly that they have come to help take them home.

3. The dying person is reassured by the experience and expresses great happiness with the vision. The dying also seem quite willing to go with these apparitions.

4. The dying person's mood, even state of health, seems to change. During these visions, a once depressed or pain-riddled person is overcome with elation and momentarily relieved of pain.

5. These experiencers do not seem to be hallucinating or to be in an altered state of consciousness. Rather, they appear to be quite aware of their real surroundings and conditions.

6. Whether or not the dying person believes in an afterlife is irrelevant; the experience and reactions are the same. (50)

Can you imagine how our world will transform for the better as more people learn – without a doubt – that life continues after the human form perishes? Sharon wrote the following to me ***on the day of her son's funeral*** ...

> "Your words have helped me feel so much better. I really do feel peace although I miss my beautiful son so much. He fought addictions for years and, as his mom, I carried his sadness and pain deep in my heart. All I ever wanted was for my boy to feel happiness and not suffer. To be free. And now he is. But I always thought that I couldn't survive if he died. *So for me to feel this peaceful today is truly amazing!"*

After learning more about the big picture of life, Jill benefited when she received bad news about her health ...

> "I ordered *Soul Proof* a few months ago and was delighted and fascinated with the information within. A few weeks ago, I was diagnosed with cancer. Interestingly, while the doctor gave the prognosis to me, I found myself calm and surrounded by what I can only describe as love. I honestly feel that reading your book helped marshal my courage and faith to deal with this crisis."

Combined afterlife evidence from firsthand experiences and clinical research is sufficient proof for many people. However, despite that data, many lay persons and scientists still don't believe. They say: 'There is no real scientific research to support the claim of life after death.'

As of 2020, that statement is no longer true ...

Category 3
Evidence from Scientific Research

Scientific research is defined as studies performed by experimenters in laboratories at an established university or institute. Again, the following criteria are required for research to be considered truly scientific: replicated, double-blinded, controlled, multi-centered, and random-ordered experiments with highly statistically significant findings published in peer-reviewed scientific journals.

Research using the criteria above is considered to be *the gold standard* in mainstream science. This level of research provides ***valid scientific proof of life after death***. However, *scientific research is the least well-known category of afterlife evidence because:*

1. Very little scientific research on the afterlife has been conducted.

2. Findings documenting life after death haven't been officially announced yet.

3. The research involves new terms that can sound like a foreign language.

4. Definitive scientific demonstrations of life after death seem too good to be true.

5. Many scientists and university professors don't personally believe that consciousness survives bodily death even though valid scientific research indicates it does.

These are very important points so I will briefly address each one ...

1. *Very little scientific research on the afterlife has been conducted.* Why?

    a. The topic is considered so controversial that it can be professional suicide for a serious scientist to research it.

    b. Traditional funding for this subject is very difficult to find. Some visionary donors have provided funds, but they receive requests to assist many causes and can't help them all.

    c. Scientists who might investigate afterlife topics fear losing existing grants and funding.

    d. Many scientists, professors, and department heads are *materialists*, that is, they don't believe in life after death. As such, researchers who might scientifically investigate the afterlife receive peer criticism and could lose their positions.

I can understand the schism between science and religion. Just several centuries ago, eminent scientists like Galileo were arrested for announcing evidence-based discoveries that the church considered heretical. Others, such as Giordano Bruno, were burned at the stake for their cosmological beliefs.

In the past, religious teachings were the primary source of information about the afterlife. Those have often been rejected by educated persons because of documented alterations in scriptures: additions, deletions, interpretations, translations, and inadvertent transcription errors. In addition, powerful church leaders and politicians held councils that decided what parts of 'God's Word' would and wouldn't be kept in holy books. Those so-called religious leaders tried to maintain power, in part, by threatening and punishing free-thinking scientists.

Fortunately, we now live in a time when afterlife evidence can allow open-minded religious / spiritual believers – including scientists – to *follow the data.*

2. *Findings documenting life after death haven't been officially announced yet.* Funding and security considerations affect when the following will occur: announcements of scientific proof of life after death, and public demonstrations of postmaterial communication technology. I will discuss these upcoming monumental events further in this chapter.

3. *The research involves new terms that can sound like a foreign language.* Those who can't or aren't willing to expand their vocabulary may thus dismiss valid research findings as baseless.

4. *Definitive scientific demonstrations of life after death seem too good to be true.* Yes, they do. But the findings from years of university-based experiments meet all the criteria for valid scientific research and responsible conclusions.

Principle investigators in the SoulPhone Project [1] agree that their *degree of certainty about afterlife keeps increasing.* Soon, others around the world will be able to do the same and enjoy similar benefits.

5. Many scientists and university professors don't personally believe that consciousness survives bodily death even though valid scientific research indicates it does. Views of these trusted scholars – who aren't aware of and / or aren't open to recent scientific findings – affect other people. Here's a recent note I received about this:

 > "*I'm dealing with a major existential crisis that has sent me downwards into a deep depression. I've always deeply believed there is life after death. But lately, I have struggled* ***with my faith. Some academics*** *and scientists say there is no afterlife and those who believe otherwise are idiots. I do not have the education or background to dispute their claims. I hoped you could help me find some proof of the afterlife.*"

Types of evidence in this category include: *limited human perception of reality; views of scientists, professors, and physicians; scientific research on evidential mediums; and postmaterial communication technology.* The first two subcategories set the stage for better understanding the university-based scientific research.

Limited Human Perception of Reality

Reports from your five senses *may make it seem* that you are just your physical body, but the collective consciousness data indicate you are much more than that. The saying 'Things are not always as they seem' came from the literary dialogue *Phaedrus* written by Plato. (51) The full quote is even more apropos for this topic: "Things are not always what they seem; the first appearance deceives many; the intelligence of a few perceives what has been carefully hidden."

Plato's observation emphasizes the importance of scientific research about afterlife and being open-minded about the findings.

Acclaimed inventor, engineer, philosopher, and mathematician Buckminster Fuller was the author of thirty books. In the documentary *Buckminster Fuller: The Lost Interviews*, he stated: "99% of who you are is invisible and untouchable." The views of quantum physicists interviewed by Lynn McTaggart, as mentioned earlier, agree with his statement.

The following statistics highlight *the brain's limited perceptual ability* that contributes to the illusion that life ends after bodily death. Even though you appear to be standing still, the earth travels at 66,000 miles per hour and completes a trip of 595,000,000 miles around the sun every year. At the same time, the earth rotates around its own axis. Why should you rely on your five senses for an accurate understanding of reality when they don't report all this planetary movement?

As Dr. Chopra stated: "Although our package of skin and bones looks very convincing, it is a mask, an illusion, disguising our true self, which has no limitations ... I am the witness, the interpreter, the Self beyond the self-image. This Self is ageless and timeless ..." (52)

Sensitive persons – those with more extrasensory perception – have gifts of seeing, hearing, feeling, and / or knowing more of reality than most people. Unless you are one of them, *you likely have been looking at life as though through a tiny pinhole instead of seeing more of what really exists.*

Part of 'what really exists' includes life after death and your loved ones who changed worlds. Those who claimed they could perceive 'departed' loved ones have sometimes been considered strange, psychotic, or even possessed. More openness about these common perceptions exists now, in part, due to increased awareness of afterlife evidence.

It's not surprising that most people can't sense postmaterial persons when you consider the following. ***On a macro scale***, the universe is vast but – without a telescope – our vision detects very little of it. Estimates for what exists in the universe include ...

- 100 to 400 billion stars like our Sun in the Milky Way
- two trillion galaxies in the universe
- star nursery nebulae, cocoons of energy, and matter with the potential to form groups of new stars

On a micro scale, it's a similar but reverse situation. As most school children know after viewing a drop of pond water through a microscope, there are entire worlds in each cell. But unaided human vision cannot see any of that. For example …

- Each of your body's *80 trillion* or more cells have smaller subunits called *organelles.*
- These, in turn, consist of molecules, atoms and subatomic particles.
- Those are made of even smaller units such as quarks, bosons, and muons.
- The smallest particles identified have *properties of both a wave and a particle* that alternately exist as an interplay between energy and matter.
- Fluctuations between supposedly solid (particle) and formless (waves) states may occur many times per second.

Physical sciences show that objects *appearing to be solid* consist primarily of space with a few tiny atoms whirring around at high speeds. For example, if the nucleus of a hydrogen molecule were the size of a marble, its single electron would be ½ mile away. ***That's a lot of space amidst seeming solidity.***

Findings from chemistry and physics also support *the interactive nature of existence.* In my undergraduate chemistry studies, our professor was trying to explain this point. He slammed his hand on the desk and exclaimed, 'When I do this, some atoms that were in my hand are now in the desk, and vice-versa.' I will never forget that moment as the implications of his statement bounced around in my mind.

Input from Scientists, Professors, and Physicians

Many well-respected scientists have posited that bodily death is not the end of life. Nobel Prize winner Max Planck, PhD, founder of quantum physics, said: "I regard consciousness as fundamental. I regard matter as derivative from consciousness. We cannot get behind consciousness. Everything that we talk about, everything that we regard as existing, postulates consciousness." (53)

Einstein proposed *the theory of relativity* that includes this formula*: **energy equals mass multiplied by the speed of light squared.*** In other words, energy and mass are interchangeable under certain conditions. *Energy and mass are not static and separate entities; they are dynamic and intermingling phenomena that overlap.*

Friedbert Karger, PhD, physicist at the Munich Max Planck Institute, extensively studied afterlife phenomena and stated: "The consciousness – or soul – of a man lives beyond the body. The body is a tool that consciousness uses. When the body dies, the soul remains … death is not an end but a transition from one state to another." (54)

In an interview with *Scientific American* in 1920, Thomas Edison stated, "Therefore, if personality exists after what we call death, it's reasonable to conclude that those who leave this earth would like to communicate with those they have left here .... I do claim that it is possible to construct an apparatus which will be so delicate that if there are personalities in another existence or sphere who wish to get in touch with us ... this apparatus will at least give them a better opportunity." Edison was working on 'The Spirit Finder' device, but passed on before it was completed. (55)

He believed in life beyond death and may have visited the next realm during an NDE-like event. After momentarily awakening from a coma just before passing on, he stated: "It is very beautiful over there."

Wilder Penfield, MD is widely considered to be the father of neurosurgery and was responsible for much of the current understanding of brain function. Like many of his medical colleagues, Dr. Penfield thought that consciousness did not exist independently of the brain. *However, after fifty years of research, he changed his mind.* As stated in *The Mystery of the Mind*:

> "I came to take seriously, even to believe, that the consciousness of man, the mind, is NOT something to be reduced to brain mechanism ... What a thrill it is, then, to discover that the scientist, too, can legitimately believe in the existence of the spirit! Possibly the scientist and the physician could add something by stepping outside the laboratory and the consulting room to reconsider these strangely gifted human beings about us. Where did the mind – call it the spirit if you like – come from? Who can say? It exists." (56)

Willis Harmon, PhD, professor emeritus at Stanford, author of *Global Mind Change*, and founder of the Institute of Noetic Sciences stated:

> "There is a tremendous amount of empirical, anecdotal, clinical, and traditional evidence suggesting that in some sense the essence of the person survives physical death ... death appears less as an extinction than as an awakening to `where one was all along.' At death, the center of awareness shifts from the physical to higher planes (with perhaps a period of confusion and / or sleepy resting in between). We don't go somewhere at death; we are already there. As this new view becomes real in our lives, fear of death disappears. We couldn't non-exist if we wanted to." (57)

David Deutsch, PhD, a leading theoretical physicist at the University of Oxford, proposed the existence of *parallel universes.* By applying the laws of quantum physics, he argued that you simultaneously live in innumerable parallel existences or states of being. You live not in a single universe, Deutsch said, but in *a vast and rich multiverse* in which other versions of yourself may live out other options you've encountered. Even after your current physical body dies, other copies of you may remain alive in other realities. This is a different kind of afterlife scenario than usual, but it is continuation of consciousness nonetheless. (58)

Regarding the survival of consciousness after bodily death, McTaggart said: "As Fritz-Albert Popp described it, when we die we experience a 'decoupling' of our frequency from the matter of our cells. Death may be merely a matter of going home or, more precisely, staying behind – returning to The Field." (59)

Melvin Morse, MD asked leading theoretical physicists about the nature of reality. Their best current understandings were described by the term *non-local reality.* In this view, time and space are not barriers to the transmission of, or interaction between, energy and information. Morse said that nonlocality was perhaps best described by a child who, after a near-death experience, called it *the really real place.*

Morse commented: "On the one hand, we have theoretical physicists who have been trying to explain to us for the past fifty years that our material world is actually based on pulsating, endless patterns of light and energy. On the other hand, we have mystics, psychics, and those who have had near-death experiences telling us that they have had a glimpse of a level of reality in which all knowledge is contained, time and space are meaningless, and is filled with a loving light." (60)

Esteemed physicist David Bohm, PhD described the most absolute nature of reality as *unified energy that undergoes constant change.* As Bohm described in his book *Wholeness and the Implicate Order,* life is best described as an enormous totality of energy in perpetual motion. Our physical world is like a tiny ripple on a vast sea of energy, a wavelike excitation from this seething energy soup.

Bohm postulated two levels of reality that coexist and overlap. The *material order* is the manifestation of energy erroneously perceived by the five senses as finite and merely physical. The *absolute or implicate order* is infinite, consists of pure energy, and transcends physicality. Together, these two aspects comprise an undivided whole that constantly flows and changes. Even 'empty space' is full of this energy that ultimately merges and unites in *a holomovement*, Bohm's term for the dynamic and holographic nature of reality.

In *The Medium, the Mystic, and the Physicist*, Lawrence LeShan, PhD stated: "It is very difficult for the modern scientist to think about the possibility of the personality surviving biological death because of his assumption that brain and mind are the same. This is accepted as the 'truth,' and it is rarely realized that this is an assumption and that other conceptualizations are possible." (61)

Scientific Research on Evidential Mediums

Can postmaterial persons communicate with us via extrasensorily gifted humans? This question has intrigued humanity for many years and differing beliefs about the answer exist.

What do replicated scientific findings say about this question? Multiple double-blinded laboratory mediumship experiments have been published over the past twenty years after research at the University of Arizona, University of Virginia, University of Glasgow, Institute of Noetic Sciences, and the Windbridge Institute. In addition, imaging studies show that different areas of mediums' brains become active when they report conversing with 'spirits' versus imagining doing so. These findings were published by Temple University, the University of Pennsylvania, and the Institute of Noetic Sciences. (62)

Before discussing this topic further, I will define some terms.

Evidential medium describes highly accurate 'sensitive' persons who can detect those who have passed on. To be considered evidential, the medium must have been evaluated by at least one independent investigator who uses controlled conditions. Genuine mediums can sometimes provide specific evidence that could not be known unless, in fact, they are communicating with postmaterial persons.

Ways of perceiving those living in nonearthly realms are described as: *clairvoyance* (clear seeing), *clairaudience* (hearing), *clairsentience* (feeling), *claircognizance* (knowing), or a combination of these.

Most evidential mediums perceive 'deceased' persons *subjectively,* that is, with their inward senses. These have been described, for example, as seeing with the mind's eye or hearing telepathically. Rarely, however, evidential mediums perceive postmaterial persons *objectively* much as they sense material persons on earth.

Many people aren't aware of the legitimacy of certain mediums because of abuse by fakes. As such, all mediums may be unfairly judged as guilty by association. Fraudulent mediums use deception, cold readings, fishing, and other unscrupulous ways to deceive clients. Some mediums provide obvious and / or very general information. For example, telling a seventy-year-old that his grandmother is 'in spirit' and loves him very much is not evidential. Gary Schwartz, PhD was a former associate professor at Harvard University and tenured professor at Yale University where he co-founded the field of behavioral medicine. He is now a senior professor at the University of Arizona where he directs research at the Laboratory for Advances in Consciousness and Health.

Dr. Schwartz has presented more than 450 scientific papers including six in the journal *Science*. He has co-edited eleven academic books, and authored or co-authored twelve additional ones. Schwartz was the founding President of the Academy for the Advancement of Postmaterialist Sciences.

Based on his research, he stated in 2019: "*Speaking as a scientist*, I am now 99.9 percent certain that life continues after bodily death." That is a very high degree of certainty, but one based on well-run replicated studies and experimental data. (63)

Dr. Schwartz and other researchers have conducted numerous studies to investigate the validity of mediums. In one study, as described in his book *The Afterlife Experiments*, he investigated five mediums and their abilities to accurately communicate with postmaterial persons. Using strict laboratory procedures, the mediums could not see or sometimes even hear subjects who hoped to receive messages from their 'deceased' loved ones. In addition, the mediums had no way of knowing *anything* about the subjects – not their names, gender, age bracket, background, city of residence, or any other details.

After reviewing his experimental research on mediums, Dr. Schwartz concluded that the information consistently relayed what could best be explained as coming from living beings. Some information was obtained before the medium ever spoke with the subject. At times, the subject disagreed with input from the medium but that input ultimately turned out to be correct. Mediums were sometimes corrected by the post-material participants.

The data, Dr. Schwartz concluded, appeared to be valid and convincing.

In his experiments, every conceivable measure was used to ensure valid readings. Other scientists, magicians, and professional documentarians with video-cameras assisted to spot any cheating. No one who observed the laboratory's multi-blinded experiments has been able to point out any critical flaws in the scientific methodology.

In addition, no rational alternative explanations have been found for the findings. Control participants with no mediumistic abilities averaged 23% accuracy versus 86% for mediums. Statistical analyses show the chance those results could have occurred randomly are at least 1 in 1 trillion. Finding a probability of chance in the 1 out of 100 or 1,000 range is the usual requirement for publishing research findings in respected journals. Results from the medium research thus reached *1 billion times the requirement for acceptance of data validity.*

Stated Dr. Schwartz, "Scientists and nonscientists alike are experiencing a test of faith: in this case, whether we can believe in the scientific method itself. Because if we are to put our faith in the scientific method, and trust what the data reveal, we are led to the hypothesis that the universe is more wondrous than imagined in our wildest flights of fancy. The totality of the findings is surprisingly consistent with the concept of life after death and what we call the 'living soul hypothesis.'" (64)

To summarize, double-blinded and triple-blinded experiments at a leading university from 1997 to 2017 showed that accurate information was often obtained from postmaterial persons via highly skilled evidential mediums. This was the first area of scientific research that clearly indicated life continues after bodily death.

The next area of scientific research may seem even more mind-blowing to you.

Postmaterial Communication Technology

In *Greater Reality Living*, Dr. Schwartz stated, "Technologies are currently being tested to demonstrate the existence of postmaterial persons and their ability to communicate with us. To date, many proof-of-concept technologies have been evaluated. We hold the firm conviction that one day soon the technologies that result from these discoveries will *allow us to communicate with those whose earthly bodies have died.*" (65)

If such research sounds crazy or impossible to you, it may help to know that at least four esteemed 20th century scientists attempted to develop a similar technology. Alexander Graham Bell tried to create a 'Telephone to the Dead.' Guglielmo Marconi, who invented the radio, attempted to develop a 'Radio to the Dead'.

In the book *Edison vs Tesla: The Battle Over Their Last Invention,* Martin and Birnes state: “Edison's little-known near-death experience formed his theory that animate life forms don't die, but rather change the nature of their composition. It is this foundational belief that drove him to proceed with *the spirit phone*. Tesla monitored Edison's paranormal work, with both men racing to create a device that picked up the frequencies of discarnate spirits ...” (66)

I will provide some background about postmaterial communication technology before saying more about this historic and ultra-exciting development. I've directed the SoulPhone Foundation and served as a research assistant for the SoulPhone Project since 2016.

After his research with evidential mediums, Dr. Schwartz continued a collegial relationship with some of them. Independently, several mediums shared messages from ‘deceased’ luminaries encouraging Dr. Schwartz to develop ‘spirit’ communication technology. Synchronicities and meaningful pieces of complex information convinced Schwartz to be open to this possibility.

In 2004, he secretly began to research different ways to capture *signals from postmaterial persons.* Based on the initial results, in 2007 he assembled a team of electrical engineers, software programmers, optical physicists, evidential mediums, and other specialists to assist his research. Their collaborative efforts detected the following *properties of postmaterial persons*:

1. ***Physicality*** as shown by:

    a. *light diminution experiment* demonstrating the ability of postmaterial persons to slow the speed of a photon or laser beam.

    b. *creating micro-air movement* in an air-tight enclosure as detected by dynamical interferometer sensors. Some mass is required, at least according to the known laws of physics, to move air molecules.

2. ***Energy*** as measured by electromagnetic field detectors

3. ***Light*** as detected in a silicon photomultiplier light-tight box using a sophisticated camera capable of detecting a single photon of light

4. ***Sound*** as measured in a sound-proof booth using an advanced microphone and oscilloscope to show amplitudes of 'spirit' voices. This work provided proof-of-concept data for future *SoulAudio* technology (see below).

5. ***Visual aspects*** as detected by expensive cameras and proprietary software that detected anomalous frames with shadows and blurring when postmaterial persons moved in front of the camera. These experiments provided proof-of-concept data for future SoulVideo technology.

In addition, the following three sets of tests were used during seven experiments using a Plasma Globe System to detect binary signals from postmaterial participants:

1. ***Operator skills tests*** to evaluate the ability of postmaterial persons to correctly perform requested tasks

2. ***Cognitive understanding tests*** to evaluate recall of earthly words and concepts. For example, postmaterial participants uniformly showed comprehension of the difference between mechanical vehicles and animals.

3. ***Personal Identification tests*** to examine recall of details when the postmaterial participants lived on earth. Examples included asking for correct Yes / No responses to questions such as: Was your mother's name Mary? Were you born in 1921? Did you write a book entitled *The Nature of Reality*?

These measurable five properties of postmaterial persons, and their mastery of the three tests, have been repeatedly demonstrated in *proof-of-concept* studies. Collectively, these experiments show that *it is feasible to create practical devices for postmaterial communication.* The challenge has been to amplify their signals while minimizing background noise detected by ultra-sensitive equipment. In 2022, Dr. Schwartz and his team are working to develop a *proof-of-practice device* to be used for client services and, eventually, usable devices and / or apps.

Six experiments with over 1,500 sessions yielded over 1 trillion bits of data from postmaterial participants. Because of the extraordinary nature of these claims, equally extraordinary evidence was required. Scientific papers on this research are listed under (9) - (12) in *References.* A seminal paper on all studies to date is being written for a different scientific journal.

Dr. Schwartz stated, "In light of the compelling evidence and rationale for such technologies, the question is no longer, 'Is spirit communication possible?' The question is now, 'What will it take to engineer a technology to make communication extremely reliable, practical, and affordable?'" (67)

The umbrella name for this emerging technology is the SoulPhone™.

Briefly, the following postmaterial communication technologies are envisioned:

- *SoulSwitch*™ will allow communication by binary (Yes / No) responses. This will be a component of the SoulKeyboard, not a commercializable device.
- *SoulKeyboard*™ will have forty or so SoulSwitches to allow *texting and typing*.
- *SoulAudio*™ is envisioned for *talking* with postmaterial persons.
- *SoulVideo*™ should enable those living on earth to *see* those who have passed on. The goal is to achieve 3-D and holographic visual images to allow an interactive experience such as that now widely used with video-conferencing.

Several exciting advances with hardware and software development have occurred in 2021. Public demonstrations of the SoulSwitch will be given as soon as funding and security issues allow. The goal of the SoulPhone Project is to provide safe, secure, reliable, and affordable 'spirit' communication devices.

I hope this summary of scientific evidence deepens your knowing that life continues after bodily death. Knowing this information can enhance many aspects of your life on earth now. You deserve to know this great news and enjoy the many wonderful benefits therein.

AFTERWORD

Many people have said to me over the years: '*If only I knew for sure* that my 'departed' loved ones are alive and well."

> ***The collective evidence now provides that certainty.***

Others have said: '*If only I could talk with my dear ones who have passed on, even for just five minutes.*'

> ***Time-tested methods now often allow meaningful perceptions of them. And emerging interdimensional communication technology should one day enable texting, talking, and seeing.***

Now you know the proof that death is not a good-bye – just a see you later. And that, my friends, makes such a huge difference during your earthly experience.

Here's an apt metaphor: when loved ones move far away, you may feel sad and miss seeing them in person. However, you know: (1) you will see them again someday and, (2) you can keep in touch via texting, calling, and video-conferencing.

The great news? You now know that (1) is true for your post-material loved ones. And, regarding (2), you can stay in touch with them now and do so even more fully in the future.

Please share this great news with others, *especially those who are searching, struggling, and suffering.* Many people don't yet know this evidence-based information that conveys so much comfort and hope.

Here is an example from Yvonne about how this evidence can help …

> My neighbor and dear friend lost his brother to suicide a few months ago. He was very sad and I didn't know how to console him. Then I thought of your *Soul Proof* website and told him about your articles. A few days later, I saw him outside: he was full of energy and smiling. *He told me how that information changed the way he thinks about life.* He shared the articles with his family. They talked about it and his dad was finally able to cry. Thank you and God bless.

I received this note from Chris …

> If not for your free radio shows, articles, and videos, I could not get through this after my daughter passed on. My mind revisits the horrible phone call and seeing her body. Your words have been the only true source of comfort. There is no way to thank you for your continued dedication, compassion and love for mommas like me who need the hope you share.

However, even after learning all the evidence, some people still do not believe in life after death. Here's a comment that falls under the category of "*I couldn't make this up if I tried*" ...

> Just read your article after afterlife. What a load of horse s–t. We live and die and that's it. How do you supposedly ***know we don't? Did you*** actually die and remember?I think not! Or was it a message from god? He's faker than Batman. You can stop with all the lies and face your fate like the rest of us. Stop putting this bulls–t out there!

The Creator and Sustainer of All Life is faker than Batman? That's one angry and fearful guy. In my experience, lack of belief in afterlife – even after learning all the evidence – is often due to one or more of the reasons listed under Resources. [J]

So there's a lot of work to be done. Thank you for reading this book and sharing this life- and world-changing information with others. *I hope you are already feeling more peace, joy, love, gratitude, and other higher-energy emotions.* ***More evolved ways of being naturally flow*** when you truly know that you and everyone else continue living after the human form dies.

I hope I have honored the sacrifices of little Mikey and Stevie who were described in the *Introduction*. My heartfelt gratitude goes to them – and my many other patients, teachers, family, and friends – who helped me discover that *life and love do not end.*

Many benefits accompany the evidence about afterlife and the nature of reality. These include a deeper knowing that you and everyone else ...

1. continue to live after the human form dies.

2. do not really 'lose' beloved people and pets after their earthly bodies perish.

3. can enjoy continued relationships with your 'departed' loved ones now.

4. are integral, infinite, and beloved parts of Source Energy / The Light.

5. receive love, support, guidance, and assistance from evolved sources variously described as angels, guides, master teachers, and higher energies.

6. can have different cyclical and perhaps simultaneous life experiences.

7. create how heavenly or hellish your life is by your thoughts, words, and deeds.

8. are interconnected in sacred ways with all people, animals, and nature.

9. have special purposes for being on this planet at this time.

In the church services of my youth, the minister ended with this Benediction: 'May your hearts and minds be filled with *the peace that passes all understanding*.' That sounded wonderful but, truthfully, my inner peace then was like a roller-coaster that depended on external circumstances. Now, at age

68, I have that peace – and much more – almost all the time *no matter what is happening to or around me.*

I hope this book helps you know *without a doubt* that life continues after bodily death. May you increasingly experience the peace that passes all understanding.

Appendix: Religious Input About Life After Death

(Note: This information was not included in Category #1 'Evidence from Firsthand Experiences' because of the reasons discussed below.)

Religious teachings about spiritual dimensions are a source of comfort and inspiration for many people. Religious input about the nature of reality, including an afterlife, may be based on *firsthand experiences of the founders of religions* since ***reportedly***: Moses met with the Lord on Mt. Sinai, Jesus saw the spirit of God descend from the heavens, Hindu yogis perceived the Divine after intense meditation, and the Buddha saw the infinity of life after enlightenment.

After attending theology school and studying the world's religions in some depth, I'm aware of ***the lack of objective evidence for religious teachings.*** Jack Miles PhD, former Jesuit priest and author of *God: A Biography*, stated: "Myth, legend, and history mix endlessly in the *Bible*, and Biblical historians are endlessly sorting them out." Buddhist scholars admit that it's not clear what is fact and what is legend about the Buddha. Hindu scholars recognize the mix of symbolic but culturally powerful aspects in their religious teachings.

Original religious teachers millennia ago likely did the best they could with limited data and observation tools of that time. Their audiences were often illiterate, thus the need for parables, metaphors, and other story-related approaches to teaching.

The amount of time elapsed since purported original religious teachings is also problematic. Islam, the most recent, surfaced in the 6th century CE / AD while Hinduism dates back nearly 4000 years ago. Oral records supposedly relayed teachings of the founders. But many scriptural scholars and historians agree that significant changes have occurred via deletions, additions, mistranslations, and varying interpretations.

As such, *religious statements about life after death are not based on scientific or clinical evidence. Nonetheless, there may be some firsthand experience evidence behind them.* Religious teachings say that life continues after death. Discussions of the unity between creation and Creator also infer a continuation of consciousness.

Contemporary evidence shows that seemingly solid and mortal humans are really timeless beings of info-energy / consciousness / awareness. Religious terms for this deathless essence of people include soul, spirit, and breath. Genesis 1:27 in the *Bible* states, "So God created man in his own image." In I Corinthians 3:16, the apostle Paul asked: "Know ye not that ye are a temple of God and that the spirit of God dwelleth in you?" Psalms 82:6 stated, "I have said, ye are Gods; and all of you are children of the most High."

O. Lazarus, in his book *Liberal Judaism and Its Standpoint,* summarized a Reform Jewish attitude toward death: "There is that within us which is immortal and it is not bounded by time and space. It is this, man's soul, as it is called, which continues, so we believe, to live after the death of the body. To it, death is but an incident of life." Kabbalistic and Mystical Judaism also believe in the immortality of the soul.

In *Discover The Power Within You,* Unity minister Eric Butterworth stated, "You can never be separated from God because you are an expression of God, the self-livingness of God." A saying in Unity notes: 'There is no spot where God is not.' Speaking of Creator, Alfred Tennyson wrote: "Closer is He than breathing and nearer than hands and feet." Meher Baba, a spiritual master from India, said: "To attain union with God is so impossibly difficult because it is impossible to become what you already are!"

The Christian mystic St. John of the Cross said: "Oh, then, soul most beautiful among all the creatures, so anxious to know the dwelling place of your Beloved (God) that you may go in quest of Him and be united with Him, now we are telling you that you yourself are His dwelling... His secret chamber and hiding place."

Quotes about our essential oneness with Creator include...

- Sufism, an esoteric branch of Islam, says: "I looked into myself and saw that I am He."
- Referring to Oneness, the Hindu Upanishads proclaim, "I am everywhere, shining forth from all beings."
- Christianity states, "The Father and I are One."
- Islam says, "All is Allah."

'God is One' and 'I Am That I Am' are other ways of stating that there is no separation from Source and, thus, no end to life. As Joel Goldsmith wrote in *The Infinite Way*, "That which I am seeking, I am." These religious and spiritual teachings agree concur with the collective scientific and clinical evidence: ***shifts beyond the earthly experience do not equal cessation of life.***

In his book *Global Mind Change,* Dr. Willis Harmon noted Aldous Huxley's discussion of the 'perennial philosophy' that exists within esoteric branches of all religions. Harmon considered these points to be compatible with science...

1. The world of matter and individual consciousness, the world of things and animals and people, is the manifestation of a divine ground within which all partial realities have their being.

2. Humans possess a double nature, a time bound ego and an eternal self. This eternal self is the spirit, the spark of divinity within the soul. It is possible for a human being to primarily identify with this divine ground and recognize one's own true nature.

3. The life of a human being on earth has one purpose: to identify with the eternal self and come to unitive knowledge of the divine ground.

These religious quotes from antiquity comment on the spiritual immortality of humans and their oneness with Creator:

- Buddhism: "Knowing that this body is like froth, knowing that its nature is that of a mirage, the disciple passes untouched by Death."

- Sikhism: "The Lord is in every heart, and within Him is my home."

- Christianity: "I have said, Ye are gods; and all of you are children of the most High."

- Hinduism: "Deep within abides another life, not like the life of the senses, escaping sight, unchanging. This endures after created things have passed away... The individual soul is nothing else in essence than universal soul."

- Judaism: "The Lord is my shepherd... Surely goodness and mercy shall follow me all the days of my life; and I shall dwell in the house of the Lord forever."

Statements by modern-day religious teachers concur with the ancients:

- "Just as a little bird cracks open the shell and flies out, we fly out of this shell, the shell of the body. We call that death but, strictly speaking, death is nothing but a change of form." - Sri Swami Satchidananda

- "I am quite confident that the most important part of a human being is not his physical body but his nonphysical essence, which some people call soul and others, personality... The nonphysical part cannot die and cannot decay because it's not physical." - Rabbi Harold Kushner

- "The body is only a garment. How many times have you changed your clothing in this life? Yet, because of this, you would not say that *you* have changed. Similarly, when you give up this bodily dress at death, you do not change. You are just the same, an immortal soul, a child of God." - Paramahansa Yogananda

- "I believe there are two sides to the phenomenon known as death: this where we live, and the other side where we shall continue to live. Eternity does not start with death. We are in eternity now." - Rev. Dr. Norman Vincent Peale

For more information on this subject, see the 'Input from Religions and Spirituality' chapter in my book *Soul Proof.*

REFERENCES

(1) Guggenheim, Bill and Guggenheim, Judy. *Hello from Heaven*. New York: Bantam Books, 1995. p. 12.

(2) Jung, Carl G. *Memories, Dreams, Reflections*. New York: Random House. 1963.

(3) Moody, Raymond. *Reunions*. New York: Ivy Books, 1993. p. 23

(4) Moody, Raymond and Pitstick, Mark. The Best of Soul-utions. Soul Proof Productions, 2000.

(5) quote from Michael Harner PhD on *Shamanism.org* home page

(6) personal communication from Don Schmidt

(7) *Sightings: The Ghost Report*. Documentary from Paramount Pictures. 1995.

(8) *Sightings* ibid

(9) Schwartz, Gary E. (2010). Possible application of silicon photomultiplier technology to detect the presence of spirit and intention: three proof-of-concept experiments. *EXPLORE: The Journal of Science and Healing* 6, pages 166-171.

(10) Schwartz, Gary E. (2011). Photonic Measurement of Apparent Presence of Spirit Using a Computer Automated System. Explore: The Journal of Science and Healing (2011) 7(2) 100-109 DOI: 10.1016/j.explore.2010.12.002

(11) Schwartz, Gary E. (2019). A computer-automated, multi-center, multi-blinded, randomized control trial evaluating hypothesized spirit presence and communication [published online ahead of print, 2019 Nov 16]. *Explore (NY)*. 2019; S1550-8307(19)30552-X. doi:10.1016/j.explore.2019.11.007

(12) Schwartz, Gary E., Woollacott Marjorie H., eds. (2019) Is Consciousness Primary? Perspectives from the founding members of the Academy for the Advancement of Postmaterialist Sciences. 2019.

(13) Freeman, Sidney. Life After Death. Commack, NY: Kroshka Books, 1998. p. 227-228.

(14) Oyler, Chris. *Go Toward the Light.* New York: Harper & Row, 1988. p.237.

(15) Binder, Bettye and Hogshire, James. Fifty Amazing Stories of People Who Have Lived Before. Boca Raton, FL: Globe, 1992. p. 8.

(16) Wilber, Ken. *No Boundary.* Boulder: Shambhala, 1985. p. 143.

(17) Ring, Kenneth and Pitstick, Mark. The Best of Soul-utions. Soul Proof Productions, 2000.

(18) Weiss, Brian. *Messages from The Masters.* New York: Warner Books, 2000. p. 168-171.

(19) Moody, Raymond. *The Light Beyond.* Bantam: New York, 1988. p.173

(20) Morse, Melvin and Perry, Paul. *Closer to the Light.* Ballantine: New York, 1990. p. 123.

(21) Ring and Cooper, *Mindsight.* Palo Alto, CA: Wm. James Center for Consciousness Studies, 1999. p.xv.

(22) Ring, Kenneth and Pitstick, Mark. *Best of Soul-utions*

(23) Grof, Stanislav. Books of the Dead. London: Thames & Hudson, 1994. p. 31.

(24) von Lommell, Pim. Near-death experience in survivors of cardiac arrest: a prospective study in the Netherlands. Lancet. 2001 Dec 15;358(9298):2039-45.

(25) Cockell, Jenny. *Across Time and Death.* New York: Simon & Schuster, 1993.

(26) Bowman, Carol. *Children's Past Lives.* New York: HarperCollins, 2001. p. 147, 332-333.

(27) Whitton, Joel and Fisher, Joe. Life Between Life. Garden City, NY: Doubleday, 1986. p. 144-156.

(28) Weiss. *Messages from The Masters,* p. 171-173.

(29) Chopra, Deepak. *How To Know God.* Harmony Books: New York. 2000. p. 234.

(30) Weiss. *Messages from The Masters.* p. 82-85.

(31) Head, Joseph and Cranston, Sylvia. *Reincarnation: The Phoenix Fire Mystery.* Pasadena, CA: Theosophical University Press, 1994. p. 401-402.

(32) Lenz, Frederick. *Lifetimes.* New York: Ballantine Books, 1979. p. 37.

(33) Holzer, Hans. *The Secret of Healing.* Hillsboro, OR: Beyond Words, 1995. p 81.

(34) Newton, Michael. *Journey of Souls.* St. Paul, MN: Llewellyn, 1994. p. 2.

(35) Wade, Jenny. *Changes of Mind.* Albany, NY: State Univ. of NY Press, 1996. p. 111.

(36) Ring and Cooper. p.182.

(37) Chamberlain, David. *Babies Remember Birth.* Los Angeles: Tarcher, 1988. p. 103-104,106, 120.

(38) Grof, Stan. *Beyond the Brain.* Albany, NY: State Univ. of New York Press, 1985. p. 39.

(39) Newton, Michael and Pitstick, Mark. *Soul Proof* documentary film. Soul Proof Productions. 2008.

(40) Clark, Ann and Pitstick, Mark personal communication on April 2, 2021
(41) Moody. *The Last Laugh.* Charlottesville, VA: Hampton Roads, 1999. p. 4 - 5.
(42) Borysenko, Joan. *Fire In the Soul.* New York: Warner Books, 1993. p. 147.
(43) Nahm, Michael. *Terminal Lucidity in People with Mental Illness and Other Mental Disability: An Overview and Implications for Possible Explanatory Models.* Journal of Near-Death Studies. 2009.
(44) Betty, Stafford. *Huffington Post* blog: *When Alzheimer's Victims Suddenly 'Perk Up' Just Before Death - What's Going On?* https://www.huffpost.com/entry/the-miracle-of-terminal-l_b_5863492. 2014.
(45) Bering, Jesse. *One Last Goodbye: The Strange Case of Terminal Lucidity.* https://blogs. scientificamerican .com/bering-in-mind/one-last-goodbye-the-strange-case-of-terminal-lucidity/. 2014.
(46) Division of Perceptual Studies at University of Virginia School of Medicine https://med. virginia.edu/perceptual-studies/our-research/types-of-cases/
(47) Wagner, Stephen. *Deathbed Visions: Are Dying People Escorted to the Other Side by Loved Ones?* ThoughtCo. com. 2017.
(48) Mendoza, Marilyn. *Deathbed Visions: Experiences of the Dying* - part 1 and 2. https://www. psychology-today.com/us/blog/understanding-grief/201610/deathbed-visions-part-i. 2016.
(49) Wills-Brandon, Carla. *One Last Hug Before I Go.* New York: Simon & Schuster. 2010.
(50) Osis, Karlis and Haraldsson, Erlendur. *At the Hour of Death.* New York: Hastings House. 1997.

(51) https://www.goodreads.com/author/quotes/889. Phaedrus

(52) Chopra, Deepak. *How To Know God.* New York: Harmony Books. 2000. p. 234.

(53) Planck, Max. Interview in *The Observer* (January 25, 1931). p.17.

(54) Karger, Friedbert. *Columbus Dispatch* (October 8 1995)

(55) Martin, Joel and Romanowski, Patricia. *We Don't Die.* New York: Berkeley Books, 1988. p. 7, 110, 276-284.

(56) Penfield, Wilder. *The Mystery of the Mind.* Princeton, N.J.: Princeton University Press, 1975. p. 85.

(57) Harmon, Willis. *The Re-emergence of the Survival Question.* Noetic Sciences Review, Winter 1994, p. 30-33.

(58) Folger, Tim. *Physics' Best Kept Secret.* Discover. Sept. 2001: 36-43.

(59) McTaggart, Lynne. *The Field.* New York: Harper, 2002. p. 33, 196.

(60) Morse, Melvin from his foreword to *The Other Side and Back* by Sylvia Browne. 2000.

(61) LeShan, Lawrence. *The Medium, the Mystic, and the Physicist.* New York: Viking Press, 1966. p. 258-259.

(62) Schwartz, Gary and Pitstick, Mark. *Greater Reality Living.* CA: Waterside Productions. 2018. p.12

(63) Schwartz, Gary and Pitstick, Mark. *Greater Reality Living.* p.11

(64) Schwartz, Gary. *The Afterlife Experiments.* New York: Pocket Books, 2002. p. vii, xviii, xxii.

(65) Schwartz, Gary and Pitstick, Mark. *Greater Reality Living.* p. 44

(66) Martin, Joel and Birnes, William. *Edison v. Tesla: The Battle Over Their Last Invention.* New York: Simon

& Schuster. 2017. from About the Book at https://www.simonandschuster. com/books/Edison-vs-Tesla/Joel-Martin/9781510718760

(67) Schwartz, Gary and Pitstick, Mark. *Greater Reality Living*. p.15

RESOURCES

(Note: articles cited are at SoulProof.com. These free articles provide my understandings about and holistic solutions for each topic. Also listed are *transformational techniques* as described at SoulProof.com/Shop. These digital audio-products cost only $15.)

[A] Board members for the *Academy for Advancement of Postmaterialist Sciences* include Drs. Larry Dossey, Dean Radin, Marjorie Woollacott, Gary Schwartz, Charles Tart, and other experts in the field of consciousness studies. *AAPSGlobal.com*

[B] How a wise and loving Creative Intelligence can coexist with suffering: articles 13, 29, 68, 78

In short, limited human perspectives and understandings cannot fathom the reasons life unfolds as it does. For example, from a myopic earthly view, Mikey and Stevie were just little children who died tragically. However, from a greater reality perspective, they may be evolved teaching souls who volunteered to temporarily suffer for the many potential positive ripples. The beneficial impacts from their brief time on earth are incalculable.

For example, when the bodies of Mikey and Stevie died in the ER, those were the only times I ever saw doctors and nurses openly weep and hug each other. The bodily deaths of those boys motivated me to search as long and hard as I have over the last 48 years. I assume they affected others as well.

[C] Continuing relationships with your postmaterial loved ones now: articles 3, 6, 9, 28

[D] Increasing chances of perceiving postmaterial loved ones: articles 9, 51, 70, 77, and 86; Facilitated After-Death Communication Technique, methods at Shamanism.org, and audio-technology at SacredAcoustics.com and Hemi-Sync.com

[E] Psychomanteum / Mirror Gazing Technique: *Reunions* book by Raymond Moody, MD, PhD.; article with 'how to' information at Gaia.com/article/psychomanteum-mirror-gazing

Induced ADCs: *Induced After-Death Communications* book by Allan Botkin, PsyD and Craig Hogan, PhD. Induced-ADC.com

Facilitated After-Death Communication Technique: article 9; Facilitated ADC Technique

[F] Spiritually Transformative Experiences: article 17; Ask Your Soul Technique

[G] Becoming a shining light versus deeply grieving person: article 82

[H] Division of Perceptual Studies at the University of Virginia's School of Medicine: Med.Virginia.edu/perceptual-studies/

[I] The SoulPhone Project is directed by Gary E. Schwartz, PhD at the Laboratory for Advances in Consciousness and Health at the University of Arizona; LACH.arizona.edu and SoulPhone.com

[J] Root causes of disbelief in life after death after learning the collective evidence:

1. *Fear of a fiery eternal hell*: nihilistic beliefs can stem from religious teachings about a fiery eternal hell. S*ome people understandably don't want there to be an afterlife* because it may be the fire-and-brimstone type. Learning more accurate and contemporary understandings about the nature of heaven and hell can help. (articles 14 and 45; Life Review Technique)

2. *Religious teachings about a vengeful God* can also make people not want to believe in an afterlife designed by such a Creator. Learning contemporary understandings about the Ground of All Being can address related fears and blocks. (article 13)

3. *Not wanting to see an abuser again* can make people hope there isn't an afterlife. Many women have expressed concerns about having to confront an abusive father or other male relative in the afterlife. Learning that they can *choose* who to see or not see removes that concern. Also, knowing that abusers may – from a big picture of life perspective – really be teachers can also help. (articles #40, 49, 67)

4. *Unresolved emotional trauma* can make an afterlife seem undesirable. People who have gone through

severe and chronic suffering may think an afterlife is wishful thinking. Or they may long for cessation of consciousness. Releasing old wounds and stuck energy with breathwork methods can help. (articles #29, 48, 70; Holistic Breathing Technique; Heal and Transform Your Suffering Technique*)*

5. *Believing life is unfair, chaotic, and meaningless* is another factor that can prevent people from seriously considering the afterlife evidence. Remember my angry shouts to God after Mikey's body died? It's helpful to learn that *people may choose,* for meaningful reasons, the possibility of difficulties. (article 25; Pre-Birth Planning Technique; Identify and Fulfill Your Purpose Technique)

6. *A superficial intellectual versus an internalized knowing* of the afterlife evidence can make it seem false. The five factors above can contribute to this problem. Re-reading and discussing the afterlife evidence can help. However, I suspect that *the level of a person's soul development* – older / advanced versus younger / beginner – affects how much people can 'really get' the great news of life after death.

If you can relate to one or more of these concerns, you have lots of company. To deepen your degree of certainty about the afterlife, I recommend using the resources listed above. If needed, seek psychological, psychiatric, and / or religious / spiritual counseling to address origins of your fears and blocks.

Some people have found that the following combination helps to internalize the great news of life after death:

1. *re-read* this book soon so you really own it

2. *discuss* the information with trusted family members and friends

3. *share* this book with others who can use it

Whatever it takes, I hope you find a way to seriously consider the wealth of evidence that proves life does not end when the human form does. You deserve to be happy, healthy, energetic, and peaceful. *Knowing that you and your loved ones don't really die is a huge key to that.* In addition, the world needs your greatest gifts and talents. Those are difficult to identify and share if you are hobbled by needless fear and limiting beliefs.

About the Author

Mark Pitstick, MA, DC, has forty-nine years' experience helping people in hospitals, pastoral counseling settings, mental health centers and holistic health care practice.

His training includes: bachelor of science degree in zoology (Ohio State University 1975); graduate theology studies majoring in pastoral counseling (Methodist Theological School of Ohio 1977 – 1978); master of arts in clinical psychology (Western Carolina University 1980); and doctorate in chiropractic health care (Palmer College of Chiropractic 1985). He also was trained in suicide prevention counseling and education.

When Mark was six years old, he told his parents that a beautiful sunset 'reminds me of God.' Mark became aware of occasional clairaudient and clairsentient abilities at age ten; he's had a number of miracles, revelatory, and spiritually transformative experiences.

After working in hospitals with many suffering and dying adults and children, he was motivated to find evidence-based answers to questions that many people ask: "Who am I? Why am I here? What happens after I die? Will I see my departed loved ones again? Is there a God? If so, why is there so much suffering? and How can I best live during this brief earthly experience?"

Dr. Pitstick wrote the books *Soul Proof, Radiant Wellness,* and *The Eleven Questions* with endorsements from Drs. Wayne Dyer, Elisabeth Kubler-Ross, Deepak Chopra, Bernie Siegel, and others. He co-authored Greater Reality Living (with Gary E. Schwartz PhD), and The Big Picture of Life (with Dr. Schwartz and Katta Mapes MA, MEd).

Mark produced the *Soul Proof* documentary film with interviews of people who had near-death experiences, after-death communications, and other eye-opening encounters. His eleven audio products use deep relaxation, breathing techniques, and guided imagery to help people deeply *know and show* they are integral, infinite, eternal, and beloved parts of Source.

A frequent media guest, Mark hosted *Soul-utions,* a radio show about practical spirituality, and *Ask the Soul Doctors* with interviews of top consciousness experts. His interviews with Brian Weiss MD, Caroline Myss MA, Michael Newton PhD, Anita Moorjani, and others can be heard at SoulProof.com/Radio Shows. Mark provides clinical support for HelpingParentsHeal.org group leaders and *Caring Listeners,* and contributes to their newsletter for bereaved parents.

Pitstick is certified in past life regression therapy by Brian Weiss MD, and the psychomanteum technique by Raymond Moody PhD, MD. Mark was the executive vice-president of Eternea.org started by Eben Alexander MD and John Audette MA. Dr. Pitstick is a member of the Institute of Noetic Sciences,

International Association for Near-Death Studies, and Academy for the Advancement of Postmaterial Sciences. He has given many workshops and webinars on spiritual awareness and holistic wellness including a twelve-part *Create the Life YOU* Envision series with ISGO (IANDS Sharing Groups Online).

Mark directs the SoulPhone Foundation that: (1.) teaches the collective evidence for life after death to people worldwide, and (2.) supports 'spirit' communication technology research and development at the University of Arizona. He is a research assistant for the SoulPhone Project at their *Laboratory for Advances in Consciousness and Health.*

Mark founded Greater Reality Living groups to help people prepare for the paradigm shift after official announcements and public demonstrations in 2022 of scientific proof of life after death. These announcements and public demonstrations will occur after completion of multicenter studies and development of an optimal SoulSwitch. To learn more about Dr. Pitstick's outreaches, visit SoulProof.com, SoulPhone.com, and GreaterRealityLiving.com.

Made in the USA
Middletown, DE
24 July 2024

57684602R00070